Supporting the Dream

*High School–College Partnerships
for College and Career Readiness*

Charis McGaughy

Andrea Venezia

Foreword by David T. Conley

CORWIN
A SAGE Company

FOR INFORMATION:

Corwin

A SAGE Company

2455 Teller Road

Thousand Oaks, California 91320

(800) 233-9936

www.corwin.com

SAGE Publications Ltd.

1 Oliver's Yard

55 City Road

London EC1Y 1SP

United Kingdom

SAGE Publications India Pvt. Ltd.

B 1/I 1 Mohan Cooperative Industrial Area

Mathura Road, New Delhi 110 044

India

SAGE Publications Asia-Pacific Pte. Ltd.

3 Church Street

#10-04 Samsung Hub

Singapore 049483

Printed in the United States of America

A catalog record of this book is available from the Library of Congress.

ISBN 978-1-4833-1681-9

Executive Editor: Arnis Burvikovs

Associate Editor: Desirée A. Bartlett

Editorial Assistant: Andrew Olson

Production Editor: Amy Schroller

Copy Editor: Tina Hardy

Typesetter: C&M Digitals (P) Ltd.

Proofreader: Dennis W. Webb

Indexer: Jean Casalegno

Cover Designer: Bryan Fishman

Marketing Manager: Lisa Lysne

This book is printed on acid-free paper.

SFI label applies to text stock

15 16 17 18 19 10 9 8 7 6 5 4 3 2 1

Supporting the Dream

Contents

Foreword

The U.S. educational system is facing an existential crisis the likes of which it has not seen for decades. Educators in the K–12 and postsecondary systems along with policymakers at the state and federal levels are asking the following question: What is the purpose of education and what is the best way to organize schooling to achieve its purpose? The last time education faced a crisis of meaning of this proportion triggered by massive changes in the macroeconomic system was at the dawn of the 20th century. Schooling was being rapidly transformed from an agrarian model, in which not all students attended school and few progressed beyond the primary level, to a model in which attendance was mandatory and where students were prepared for life in an industrial society and economy.

The 20th century model had as a defining feature the fact that schools made a choice about the futures of students. The choice was between college and work. The proportion choosing college grew consistently throughout the century and then increased dramatically in the 1980s and 1990s. Vocational programs remained in most schools, but they began to be replaced by career and technical education courses that connected to postsecondary certification programs.

Even though the number and percentage of students going on to college increased consistently, the basic relationships between high schools and colleges did not change in many ways. The types of colleges students attended expanded, with more students choosing two-year institutions that offered technical training programs and certificates. By and large, though, students did not have new options. They were still routed onto a college-prep track, into a vocational-technical program, or left dangling in the limbo of the general education track.

Much of the increase in the proportion of students going on to college that was occurring in the waning years of the 20th century accelerated during the opening decade of the 21st century and continues to gain momentum. Tracking students into programs leading to distinctly different futures continues to lose favor because it is viewed as inequitable and inflexible. In place of tracking are models designed to have all students reach a level of knowledge and skill necessary to pursue baccalaureate degrees and career-training programs. These new programs build on many efforts that have been around for decades and have helped some high school students make the transition to college more seamlessly. These programs focus on academic preparation or readiness for career training and are more rigorous and demanding than in past practice. Examples include Advanced Placement (AP), International Baccalaureate (IB), concurrent enrollment, career and technical education (CTE), and high school-to-college bridge programs, among many others.

Some postsecondary institutions have increased their efforts to communicate with secondary schools by sending more information on college freshman student performance back to high schools, by embedding college-created assessment questions in state high school exams to help signal students on their level of college readiness, by initiating more programs to connect high school students with college earlier, and by creating opportunities for college students to work in schools as interns or mentors. Additionally, a great deal of research on what it takes to be ready to succeed in entry-level college courses has been conducted over the past 15 years. These findings help schools and postsecondary institutions better align high school courses with the expectations students will encounter in college.

Many state assessments are now designed to gauge college and career readiness to a greater degree. Items on a revised version of the SAT that will be implemented in 2016 will be more reflective of the reading, language, and analytic skills students use in college. The two assessments designed to measure the college and career readiness level of the Common Core State Standards, Smarter Balanced and Partnership for Assessment of Readiness for College and Careers (PARCC), will also provide additional information on students' English and math skills.

States have adopted policies to emphasize the importance and centrality of college and career readiness and to help ensure that more students are ready to succeed in college. Examples include California's Early Assessment Program, which lets 11th graders know whether they are ready for college-level coursework, and the Texas College and Career Readiness Initiative, which is discussed in this book.

Educational governance and finance, however, for the most part, still remain frozen in a 20th- or 19th-century model, with entirely separate systems for K–12 and postsecondary education. This makes it exceedingly difficult to coordinate or fully align curricula, teacher learning, student supports, and college and career readiness programs in ways that enable all students to be ready to succeed in some form of postsecondary study. The separation of secondary and postsecondary systems requires school districts and schools to come up with strategies to improve alignment with a statewide policy framework that may not be designed to facilitate harmonious relations between systems. In other words, to support higher levels of learning for a larger proportion of students, secondary and postsecondary educators need to work together; one system cannot solve the problems of separate systems in isolation from the other.

Local solutions can be tailored to local needs and can be owned to a much greater degree by educators at both levels and, consequently, will likely affect students more than do state policies in this area. For example, stakeholder meetings to identify or agree on key knowledge and skills needed for college readiness and success can help faculty in both educational systems understand more deeply what each needs to do to help students make successful transitions. Programs designed to provide socioemotional supports for specific groups of students can help increase both student success and the diversity of the college population locally or statewide. Courses taught in high school for college credit can be mutually beneficial if high school and college faculty can agree on a means to ensure course quality. Classroom visitations can be powerful experiences—both for college instructors who visit high school classes and for high school teachers who get to spend time on a local college campus observing practices in a college classroom.

Given the tendency of schools to look to one another for solutions, experimentation takes on great importance in education. Someone needs to go first, much like the 1970s commercial for Life cereal in which two young children feed the cereal to their younger brother first before trying it themselves, and, in the process, discover, "He likes it! Hey, Mikey!" Educators innovating to find new, local solutions to alignment are in the Mikey role at the moment, while many of their colleagues stand back to see if Mikey approves.

This book is designed to serve as a framework and guidebook for educators who seek to experiment and take steps toward partnerships that improve college and career readiness for a large proportion of students. The change process is predicated on several core beliefs and principles—that all students are capable of continuing their education beyond high school, that secondary school should be oriented toward this goal, and that postsecondary and secondary education colleagues need to work together to make this happen. Key components include actions that ensure students have the necessary knowledge, skills, abilities, and dispositions to be successful after high school. The Four Keys model discussed in the book frames the necessary facets of readiness that schools need to address and students need to achieve. Nothing about this process of change is necessarily easy. However, the need is compelling, and the ultimate goal is worthy. The end result will be more citizens who are capable of leading productive, fulfilling lives in which they are able to adapt to the inevitable changes and challenges they will face during their lifetime.

David T. Conley

Preface

College and career readiness currently headline educational policy agendas in states across the country and at the federal level, yet the specific actions necessary to achieve this goal for a larger proportion of students are not clear. This can put great pressure on local schools and postsecondary institutions, since they are being asked to support new trajectories for a large proportion of their students, yet they are often provided little guidance about how to do so. Local and regional partnerships between high schools and colleges are being developed in communities and regions across the country to help improve students' readiness for colleges and careers, but many lack frameworks and tools to help structure the work and create new opportunities for students. In addition, many local and regional partnerships rely on funding and support from various sources with different aims, which often fragments their work and makes it challenging to have an overarching set of goals and objectives.

What Are Educational Partnerships and Who Is the Audience for This Book?

A partnership, in this book, is defined as a group of representatives from, at minimum, one K–12 educational institution and at least one postsecondary institution, working together to improve college and career readiness within a community. Partnerships can also be much larger in scope and can encompass an entire region; within the region, relationships must be developed among individual school districts and postsecondary institutions. These local partnerships are also referred to throughout the book as vertical teams. These vertical teams work to transcend boundaries, increase alignment, and narrow the gaps between the secondary and postsecondary systems.

Several additional stakeholders can be included in the partnerships, including other educational institutions located in the region and community-based, philanthropic, civic/governmental, business, labor, or parent organizations from the community. This book aims to inform and support the work of K–12/postsecondary partners at the regional and local levels.

How Will This Book Help Educators?

Absent clear and actionable information about how to develop and implement reforms to support student success after high school, the current rhetoric can sound hollow. This book contains resources that are designed to help equip both K–12 and postsecondary educators with strategies and tools to improve college and career readiness for all students. There is no one-size-fits-all model or template for this work, and going through the collaborative process of developing frameworks and materials is a critically important part of the development, engagement, and buy-in stages for any partnership. At the same time, these partnerships are comprised largely of volunteers who do not have the time to reinvent the wheel. An objective of this book is to provide information that can be tailored for specific partnership needs, enabling the educators involved in partnerships to use research-based information and save time by not starting from scratch. We understand that K–12 educators are often churning in a swirl of constant change, with reforms cycling in and out and often back in again. Often, the tendency is to duck and cover and wait for reforms to blow over. The research, strategies, and tools discussed in this book, while consistent with the current college and career readiness focus of many reforms, are grounded in what we know about students' aspirations (the vast majority want to continue some kind of learning after high school), their chances of earning a living wage (which are boosted by postsecondary education or training), and the realities of our disconnected educational systems. We acknowledge that there are a host of other reasons why students do not learn well in high school and in college, such as those related to personal and family issues. This book does not address those kinds of supports.

What Is the Basis for This Book?

All of the conclusions, recommendations, and strategies contained in the book are based in, and supported by, research and practice. The authors have over 40 years of combined experience working directly within the field of K–16 reform—in both policy and practice at the federal, state, and local levels and in both K–12 and postsecondary education environments. They have conducted applied research and provided technical assistance for postsecondary institutions, secondary schools, school districts, state and federal governments, national nongovernmental organizations, and national- and state-level philanthropic foundations. McGaughy has conducted several dozen partnership workshops all over the country and directed multiple statewide college and career readiness-related initiatives. In 2013–2014, Venezia was a member of Sacramento's Pathways (P–16) Initiative—a position that provided her with a unique lens that straddled the line between researcher and practitioner. Also, her center, EdInsights, runs projects focused on conducting research on, and technical assistance for, regional partnerships, and she teaches about student supports that span K–12 and postsecondary education systems. The purpose of this book is to translate the authors' collective research and professional experiences into actionable steps—including frameworks, examples, and techniques—to support the work that educators are doing across systems to support student success.

How Is This Book Organized?

The first chapter provides information about the research behind and rationale for the work; the intent is for the references to literature and context that are presented here to be used for stakeholder buy-in, proposals, or meeting materials to help make the case for cross-system work. The remaining chapters describe components of a process, including suggested strategies, tools, and techniques, to develop and sustain local partnerships to improve college and career readiness (absent a discussion about fundraising, which, though critical, is very context specific). Chapter 2 provides a conceptual framework to organize the work to ensure a comprehensive, not piecemeal, approach. Chapter 3 describes a process for organizing a local partnership, including establishing key stakeholder involvement, creating a vision and goals, and selecting an organizational structure. Chapter 4 discusses how to measure success and provides multiple examples of indicators for college and career readiness and success. Chapter 5 details the categories of programming and activities that the partnership can implement; it also provides a mapping strategy to help ensure that all students have an opportunity to learn the knowledge and skills and receive the supports they need to be successful beyond high school. Chapter 6 offers a step-by-step guide for how vertical teams of high school and postsecondary faculty members can collaborate to create an aligned curriculum across their systems. Chapter 7, the final chapter, addresses how to sustain partnership efforts, including examples and a discussion of how to avoid predictable barriers. Given McGaughy's extensive work at the Educational Policy Improvement Center (EPIC), the framework for this book is based on the Four Keys to College and Career Readiness model developed by David Conley, founder of EPIC (discussed in Chapter 2).

Acknowledgments

This book was made possible by the support and collaboration of many generous colleagues from around the country. Most significantly, we owe deep gratitude to Dr. David Conley, the founding CEO of the Educational Policy Improvement Center (EPIC), for his pioneering and visionary leadership in advancing the field of college and career readiness and for providing the conceptual framework used in this book. In addition, several state educational agencies around the country invested in much of the partnership work described in this book, including the Massachusetts Department of Elementary and Secondary Education, the Texas Higher Education Coordinating Board, the Texas Education Agency, the Illinois State Board of Education, the Illinois Community College Board, the Illinois Board of Higher Education, the Connecticut Board of Regents for Higher Education, and the California Community College Chancellor's Office. It is not possible to name all of the individuals involved across the country in both statewide and regional partnership activities contributing to this book, but a special thanks to some of the key thought partners is necessary, including Susan Wheltle, Stafford Peat, Dr. Raymund Paredes, Evelyn Hiatt, Lynette Heckman, Dr. Kristen Kramer, Malia Sieve, Michael Meotti, Dr. Braden Hosch, Brian Durham, Debbie Meisner-Bertauski, Dr. Joann Kantner, Dr. Elaine Johnson, Dr. Bob Blankenberger, and Sonia Ortiz-Mercado.

This book was also made possible by the tireless efforts of our colleagues over the past eight years at EPIC. Holly Langan and Kirsten Aspengren provided unwavering support no matter the time or situation. We also thank Mary Martinez, Tris O'Shaughnessy, Eve Gray, Jennifer Forbes, Katie Cadigan, Brittney Young, Terri Ward, and a host of others, and the later road warrior days with Adrienne van der Valk, Rachel Farkas, and Teresa Zalewski Whyte, deserve the highest praise for their dedication and outstanding work. It has been an honor and pleasure to work with these individuals toward our shared mission of improving high school and postsecondary opportunities for all students.

We also need to offer our heartfelt gratitude to our editors and reviewers. We thank Arnis Burvikovs and Desirèe Bartlett for their patience and vast editorial expertise and the rest of the team—Andrew Olson, Amy Schroller, Bryan Fishman, and Tina Hardy—for helping us publish this book. We also thank our reviewers for their thoughtful feedback that led to a stronger manuscript.

Publisher's Acknowledgments

Corwin gratefully acknowledges the editorial insight and guidance from the following reviewers:

Judy Brunner
Author, Consultant,
  Clinical Faculty
Instructional Solutions Group &
  Missouri State University
Springfield, MO

Dave Daniels
High School Principal
Susquehanna Valley Senior
  High School
Conklin, NY

Brian Durham, Senior Director
Academic Affairs & Career and
  Technical Education
Illinois Community College
  Board
Springfield, IL

Todd Hurst
Director of Education and
  Workforce Innovation
Center of Excellence in
  Leadership of Learning at the
  University of Indianapolis
Indianapolis, IN

Kristen Kramer, Senior
  Director
College Readiness and Success
  Initiatives
Austin, TX

Alice Manus
Assistant Principal
Soldan International Studies
  School
Fenton, MO

Curt Rees
School Principal
School District of Onalaska
Onalaska, WI

Natalie B. Schonfeld, Director
Student Transition Services
University of California, Irvine
Irvine, CA

David Tebo
Superintendent
Hamilton Community Schools
Hamilton, MI

About the Authors

**Dr. Charis McGaughy** has worked within the educational arena for over two decades. She recently began serving as the chief of staff for the Eugene School District 4J. Prior to that, she was a director at the Educational Policy Improvement Center (EPIC) for almost eight years. During her tenure, she worked all over the country on national, state, and district-level initiatives related to improving college and career readiness and increasing secondary and postsecondary alignment. She has also worked at the state level for the Texas Education Agency and the Tennessee Department of Children Services. She began her career as a teacher and has taught in the Houston Independent School District and in Boston Public Schools. Dr. McGaughy has considerable experience directing large-scale, multifaceted educational policy initiatives, is an experienced public speaker, and is the author of several reports, chapters, and articles on education. Her background as an educator and an educational policy worker and her extensive research experience enable her to serve as a bridge among various educational stakeholder groups. Dr. McGaughy holds a PhD in educational leadership, policy, and organizations from Vanderbilt University, an MA in public affairs from the LBJ School of Public Affairs at the University of Texas at Austin, and a BA in government from Pomona College.

 **Andrea Venezia** is executive director of the Education Insights Center (EdInsights): Advancing Research and Policy for K–12 and Postsecondary Education and associate professor in the Public Policy and Administration Department at California State University, Sacramento. Her work focuses on improving student readiness for, and success in, some form of postsecondary education—particularly for students who are traditionally underserved. Before she joined Sacramento State, Venezia worked at WestEd and oversaw a line of work focused on such issues as high school reform, state and federal policy with regard to college and career readiness, and community college readiness and success. Prior to joining WestEd, Venezia was senior policy analyst at the National Center for Public Policy and Higher Education. Before that, she directed Stanford University's Bridge Project, the first large-scale national study that documented state policy barriers inhibiting student progression from high school to college. Prior to those positions, Venezia worked in a variety of state, federal, and nonprofit organizations, including the Texas Higher Education Coordinating Board, the Charles A. Dana Center at the University of Texas at Austin, the U.S. Department of Education, the National Education Goals Panel, and the American Institutes for Research. She has authored, coauthored, and coedited numerous reports, chapters, articles, and books, including *Minding the Gap: Why Integrating High School with College Makes Sense and How to Do It* (2007), published by Harvard Education Press, and *From High School to College* (2004), published by Jossey-Bass. She received a BA in English from Pomona College, an MA in administration and policy analysis in higher education from Stanford University, and a PhD in public policy from the Lyndon B. Johnson School of Public Affairs at the University of Texas at Austin.

None of this would have been possible without the unconditional love and generous support from our families. Jeff and Dan are incredible life partners who took on extra family responsibilities so that we could complete this book; Maya, Jolie, Anika, and Sander are the ultimate inspirations driving our work. And an extra special thanks goes out to our parents who made us aware of educational inequalities; we can never begin to repay them for all they have done for us and for our families.

Understanding College
and Career Readiness

To improve college and career readiness, the concept itself must be clearly understood. This book uses the terms "college" and "postsecondary education" interchangeably, but there is a critically important difference. "College" connotes a four-year liberal arts education to many people, even though community colleges provide a great deal of career and technical training. Most of the resistance against providing a larger proportion of students with readiness for postsecondary education comes from people who are concerned that these efforts will shoehorn all students into a traditional four-year degree path. "Some form of postsecondary education" is the focus of this book; it connotes some kind of additional education or training after high school, including degrees, certificates, the military, and additional training that is neither a degree nor a certificate. To have a family-sustaining wage with the ability to move up a career ladder, most people need some kind of additional postsecondary education and/or applied training. The focus of this book is that every high school graduate should be prepared to succeed in the postsecondary environment to which they aspire. The phrase "postsecondary readiness" is somewhat clumsy and thus this book interchanges terms, but we wish to make the meaning and intent clear from the onset.

With the emergence of the concept of college and career readiness in states, regions, localities, and at the national level, many states and organizations are developing definitions of college readiness, career readiness, or both. This book utilizes the definition developed at the Educational Policy Improvement Center (EPIC), based on research on this topic over the past two decades. EPIC's definition of college and career readiness follows:

> Students who are ready for college and career can qualify for and succeed in entry-level, credit-bearing college courses leading to a baccalaureate degree, a certificate, or career pathway-oriented training programs, without the need for remedial or developmental course work. They can complete such entry-level, credit-bearing courses at a level that enables them to continue in the major or program of study they have chosen. (Conley, 2013, p. 51)

A student is college and career ready if he or she has the knowledge and skills necessary to successfully transition to the next step in his or her desired career or educational pathway. Such readiness includes both academic and nonacademic knowledge and skills (discussed in Chapter 2).

Another important distinction is the difference between college versus career readiness. Every distinct career pathway and college degree require knowledge, skills, and abilities that are unique to that area. According to research, however, college readiness and career readiness share many important elements, including study skills, time-management skills, persistence, ownership of learning, problem solving, collecting and analyzing information, and communicating in a variety of ways (Conley & McGaughy, 2012). Think of a Venn diagram. The first circle represents the college readiness knowledge and skills and student needs. The second circle represents the career readiness knowledge and skills. The intersection and overlap between the two circles represent the knowledge and skills all students need when they graduate high school. The outlying areas represent the knowledge and skills that are unique to their specific postsecondary and career fields. College and career readiness, then, represent the intersection: the knowledge, skills, and abilities that all students need to make the next step, without remediation, along their desired career pathway.

> A student is college and career ready if he or she has the knowledge and skills necessary to successfully transition to the next step in his or her desired career or educational pathway.

History

The focus on systemic reforms to connect K–12 and postsecondary education started in the last decade of the 20th century. Prior to that, most of the efforts in the field were focused on programmatic responses, such as the development of precollege outreach programs, to support traditionally underserved students. Those efforts had their origins in the Great Society reforms of the 1960s and were critically important, but awareness grew that (a) getting students *into,* but not *through,* postsecondary education was insufficient, and (b) disconnected education systems cause problems for many students.

What is the research base behind this definition? The significance of this definition is that it is both measurable and actionable. Research, policy, and practice can all be informed by answering a critical question: *What are the knowledge and skills students need to be successful in entry-level training programs, the military, or credit-bearing college courses?* Staff at EPIC has spent the past decade researching these critical questions and has established a considerable research base documenting these knowledge and skills. EPIC has collected and analyzed thousands of course documents and instructor ratings about the importance and applicability of knowledge and skills necessary for success in entry-level college courses in general education and in career and technical education (CTE) areas in both two- and four-year institutions of higher education (please refer to www.epiconline.org/publications for a complete listing of the research).

In the 1990s and early 2000s, research in this field focused on informing educators, policymakers, and the public about how the students who need the most supports in K–12 and postsecondary education often get the least (Venezia, Kirst, & Antonio, 2003) and that the sense of belonging and belief in oneself as "college material" is often lacking in first-generation college goers (McDonough, 1997). Research at that

College readiness and career readiness share many important elements, including study skills, time-management skills, persistence, ownership of learning, problem solving, collecting and analyzing information, and communicating in a variety of ways.

time also pointed to the tiers or tracks of educational offerings in middle schools, high schools, and broad access postsecondary institutions that reinforce inequalities and make it impossible for a large proportion of students to reach the American Dream through educational means (Oakes, 2005). The United States has set up systems that act as though they support educational and economic mobility, but to fulfill those aspirations across our disconnected educational systems, students need that special person who helps them navigate. The systems themselves are not set up to catch and hold the students who need help the most and provide them with the educational, motivational, psychological, and behavioral supports to lay the groundwork for successful adulthood. Each system has its own ways of helping students, but there is little that spans systems, and for students who attend more than one postsecondary institution—the vast majority of students in college—they are usually on their own to navigate, often by reaching out to extremely understaffed student services offices.

Fast forward to today and "college and career readiness" are mantras in states across the country and in the nation's capital. The Common Core State Standards (Common Core) were adopted in most states. The rhetoric of today often risks masking the core reasons for the efforts and the difficulties in making success after high school a reality for traditionally underserved students. Backlashes against the Common Core are growing, and the original hope of the "K–16 reform movement" could be lost if educational reform efforts shift focus to another issue.

> The rhetoric of today often risks masking the core reasons for the efforts and the difficulties in making success after high school a reality for traditionally underserved students.

In response to research about disconnected systems and to political pressure and many grant opportunities that require the development of cross-system governance entities, regional and local P–16 councils have sprouted up across the country. P–16 councils are collaborative teams that are formed to create a unified educational system from preschool through postsecondary education or to focus on a key issue or issues related to high school-to-college transitions. These councils usually focus on issues related to college and career readiness, such as counseling and supports, curricular alignment, and workforce preparation" (Moore, Venezia, & Lewis, 2015).

Ensuring that the local partnerships spur reforms that affect students' lives and are not just forums for people to update each other about their respective systems' efforts is the focus of this book. A key issue here is that the experiences and expectations in K–12 must education be directly connected—or scaffolded, to use the language of educators—to expectations in postsecondary education and in the workforce.

> Ensuring that the local partnerships spur reforms that affect students' lives and are not just forums for people to update each other about their respective systems' efforts is the focus of this book.

Connecting to workforce needs is not meant to imply that students should get educated just to become workers or that students should be in different curricular tracks that relegate some students to lucrative and flexible careers and others to minimum wage for life. We are strong supporters of (and have each benefitted from) excellent liberal arts education in high school and college. If liberal arts training—the abilities to think critically, analyze information, question assumptions, synthesize ideas, and so forth—is lost in a race to provide technical training too early, we believe that we will be left intellectually poorer, and the risks regarding tracking traditionally underserved students into old forms of vocational education are large. At the same time, it is clear that many students are not engaged by traditional approaches and that promising hybrids that infuse technical knowledge and experiences with strong abilities to think, analyze, synthesize, and so forth are being developed to create high-level, applied, learning opportunities for all students. Those experiences must be personalized; they are dependent on students' interests and educational strengths and weaknesses. Such efforts can be seen in California's Linked Learning and Career Pathways Trust initiatives, in Chicago's and New York's P-TECH schools, in Jobs for the Future's Pathways to Prosperity initiative, and many others across the country.

So what does this all mean in the context of this book? This book sits squarely in the center of these tough conversations that focus on some of the hardest educational issues in our country—issues around the meaning of public education, about access and equity, and about relationships between K–12 and postsecondary education.

> If readers take nothing else from this book, we hope that educators at all levels understand that working together across systems is not merely a technical issue that can be completed successfully by using specific tools and strategies or by meeting around a table together once or twice a month. This is also not simply about aligning policies at the state level or all getting on the same page about expectations at the national level.

While those efforts can help send clear signals and create coherent policy environments, this is about doing good work collaboratively and collectively across systems locally and regionally. This book is for the individuals that work directly with students on a daily basis—the people who have the power to transform individual students' lives. The work to connect systems is often more challenging than it seems like it should be, with different terminology, incentive structures, funding streams, politics, and so forth. Few people are paid to wake up in the morning and think about how to connect educational systems, and most of us are not explicitly rewarded, professionally, for doing so.

College "versus" Career Readiness

As a predictable part of a healthy policy cycle, issues related to college and career readiness are currently receiving increased scrutiny and, in some quarters, strong pushback. One of the largest critiques of the issue is the concern that not everyone should or needs to go to college (such as Owen & Sawhill, 2013; Rosenbaum, Stephan, & Rosenbaum, 2010; Samuelson, 2012). As mentioned earlier, the concern is that focusing on "college readiness" equates to a singular focus on obtaining four-year bachelor's degrees and not the plethora of pathways available for success beyond high school. Some careers require a college degree; others do not, but they do require training (and some of that is highly technical). What all of the commentators seem to agree on, and is consistent with the messaging of this book, is that everyone needs some kind of education and/or training after high school to have a successful and productive life. This is why throughout this book, the terms "college and career readiness" and "postsecondary readiness" are used interchangeably. The goal of this book is not to prepare all students to incur massive debt attending a selective university to obtain a four-year degree, but to enable communities to work together to prepare students to be successful in whichever post-high school setting to which the students aspire.

> The goal of this book is not to prepare all students to incur massive debt attending a selective university to obtain a four-year degree but to enable communities to work together to prepare students to be successful in whichever post-high school setting to which the students aspire.

This book supports the conclusion of Harvard's Pathways to Prosperity report, "The message is clear: in 21st Century America, education beyond high school is the passport to the American Dream" (Symonds, Schwartz, & Ferguson, 2011, p. 2). Students need to be able to learn well and succeed in whatever setting they choose beyond high school. What is emerging from research is that college and career readiness share many important elements, but they are not exactly the same. There is a foundational set of knowledge and skills that all high school graduates need for success beyond high school, but the precise set of knowledge and skills students need is influenced significantly by the next step they intend to take, with various career areas, institutions, and certificate or degree programs requiring proficiency in different content knowledge (Conley & McGaughy, 2012). College and career readiness represent the shared knowledge, skills, and abilities everyone needs, and the additional knowledge and skills individual students need are dependent on the specific career area, admissions, degree, certificate, and/or training requirements. Communities should work together to provide the following:

> A program of instruction at the secondary school level should therefore be designed to equip all students with the full range of necessary foundational knowledge and skills and help them set high aspirations and identify future interests . . . . Readiness is a function of the ability to continue to learn beyond high school, and particularly in postsecondary courses relevant to students' goals and interests, as represented by their choice of major or certificate program. (Conley, 2013, p. 51)

The very process of obtaining a high school diploma should keep the doors open for students, not close the ability for students' to access some career pathways.

Rationale

During a college readiness workshop sponsored by the California Community College Chancellor's Office in 2011, a group of community college admissions counselors gathered to discuss college and career readiness issues. One counselor from a Northern California community college shared a story that resonated with the participants. She described a recent meeting she had with a new student and the student's parents. The parents started the meeting by describing how proud they were of their daughter. She was the first person in their family to attend college. They had requested the meeting with the college admissions counselor because they were confused by the placement test score information the daughter had received. They had many questions, such as the following: What are placement tests? What is developmental education? Why do they have to pay for the developmental education courses since their daughter would not receive credit toward her two-year degree? The parents left the meeting upset. Their daughter had worked very hard in high school, passed all of her classes, and met all of her graduation requirements. The family kept asking, "What did we do wrong?"

Lack of academic preparedness for college is a stark reality nationwide. About 60 percent of students entering two-year colleges and nearly 20 percent of those entering four-year universities are placed in remedial courses (Bailey & Cho 2010), but it is hard to get accurate estimates because remediation is measured differently everywhere and, in some places such as California and Florida, community college students can choose not to take remedial courses, even if they receive a recommendation from their colleges to do so. Some community colleges have remediation rates of over 90 percent of their entering students, and 70 percent is not uncommon. Even four-year universities with relatively stringent entrance requirements have large numbers of students who need additional academic support; approximately half of the incoming students in The California State University (CSU) system require remediation. This is particularly troubling in the CSU system, since all entering students must have completed a college preparatory curriculum in high school and earned a B or better for their overall GPA (www.calstate.edu/eap/). Remediation serves as a serious hurdle for degree and certificate completion in college; students requiring remediation graduate at substantially lower rates. Bailey and Cho (2010) explained the remediation "pipeline" as follows:

> To take math developmental education as an example, 28 percent of those referred did not enroll. Another 30 percent failed or withdrew from one of the developmental courses in which they enrolled. Ten percent dropped out of their developmental sequences without ever failing a course. Thus, only 31 percent successfully completed their sequences of math remediation. Of those completers, about half (16 percent of all of those referred) actually completed a college-level course in math within three years. (p. 2)

This inability to place into credit-bearing entry-level college courses represents a significant barrier for attaining educational and career aspirations.

The same preparedness issues plague other arenas. In a national survey, employers reported a "skills shortage" for the U.S. workforce (Casner-Lotto & Benner, 2006). Table 1.1 lists the top skill deficiencies for high school graduates as reported by the results of a national sample of employers.

In addition to skills deficiencies for entering the workforce, many high school graduates who aspire to join the military also lack the requisite preparedness. To qualify for military service, potential recruits must meet the minimum score for their desired branch (each branch sets its own score) on the Armed Forces Qualification Test (AFQT). Between 2004 and 2009, 23 percent of the test-takers in the sample did not achieve a qualifying score (at least 31 out of 99).

Table 1.1   Skill Deficiencies of New Workforce Entrants for High School Graduates

Skill Deficiencies	Percentage of Employer Respondents
Written Communications	81
Professionalism/Work Ethic	70
Critical Thinking/Problem Solving	70
Oral Communications	53
Ethics/Social Responsibility	44
Reading Comprehension	38
Teamwork/Collaboration	35
Diversity	28
Information Technology Application	22
English Language	21

For African American candidates, 39 percent did not qualify, and for Latino candidates, the rate of ineligibility was 29 percent (Offenstein, Moore, & Shulock, 2010).

New Economic Reality

Improving college and career readiness enables students to achieve their aspirations. Whereas approximately 88 percent of eighth-grade students report that they aspired to attend college (Venezia et al., 2003), only 44 percent directly enter college after high school (National Center for Education Statistics [NCES], 2008). Without some additional education, including short-term training, simply earning a high school diploma solidifies someone's place as a low-wage earner or as part of the unemployed. While there are many stories circulating in the media about high tech geniuses who shirked college and made millions in Silicon Valley, those people had several unique factors in their favor. They were expert in a particular area—technological innovation—that also required levels of math proficiency, motivation, and persistence that many do not have. To imply that what happened to them is replicable for thousands of other people is disingenuous. Moreover, the knowledge and skills discussed in this book as prerequisites for success after high school are consistent with the experiences of many tech whizzes—to support individualized and high levels of inquiry, innovation, creativity, motivation, and resiliency.

For most students graduating from high school now, a diploma simply does not afford the same opportunities it did up until the end of the 20th century. Most professions, particularly those offering clear advancement opportunities, require some formal training beyond high school. Workers can no longer learn a single skill set and expect to secure lifetime employment relying solely on that same skill set at a life-sustaining wage. Research predicts that by 2018, 63 percent of all jobs in the United States will require some postsecondary education, and 90 percent of new jobs in growing industries with high wages will require some postsecondary education (Carnevale, Smith, & Strohl, 2010). This reality does not mean that every high school graduate should complete four years of college. What it does indicate is that stopping at high school is not sufficient to ensure access to a career with a family-sustaining wage.

> Workers can no longer learn a single skill set and expect to secure lifetime employment relying solely on that same skill set at a life-sustaining wage.

Not only are future job prospects tied to a higher skilled workforce, current job opportunities are also linked to levels of training. For example, one study found that from 2006 to 2011, only 3 in 10 recent high school graduates were employed full time, compared to college graduates who are employed at nearly twice that rate (Van Horn, Zukin, Szeltner, & Stone, 2012). From the start of the Great Recession in 2007 through 2012, people with bachelor's degrees gained over two million jobs. Those with an associate degree or some college emerged from the recession with almost the same number of jobs available as at the beginning. The group experiencing the most devastating job losses were those for workers with a high school diploma or less, losing almost six million jobs during that time period with no sign of recovery (Carnevale, Jayasundera, & Cheah, 2012). Over the past three decades, all of the net job growth in America has been generated by positions that require at least some postsecondary education (Symonds et al., 2011).

In addition to increased opportunities, increased education, on average, translates to higher earnings. The Georgetown University Center on Education and the Workforce, in the report entitled "The College Payoff" (Carnevale, Rose, & Cheah, 2011), examined lifetime earnings for all education levels and earnings by occupation, age, race/ethnicity, and gender. The results were clear: a college degree is key to economic opportunity, conferring substantially higher earnings on those with credentials than those without (Carnevale et al., 2011). See Figure 1.1 for the median lifetime earnings by the highest level of educational attainment.

The report further clarifies, however, that individual earnings vary greatly depending on the degree type, age, gender, race/ethnicity, and occupation. For example, about 28 percent of workers with associate degrees earn more than the median earnings of workers with bachelor's degrees (Carnevale et al., 2011, p. 3). What this does indicate, however, is that overall, the more education a person obtains, the potential for obtaining higher lifetime earnings increases.

A hallmark of our 21st century economy is rapid change, requiring a flexible and adaptable workforce able to create and sustain innovations and adapt to ever-changing needs. For example, former Intel Corporation Chairperson Craig Barrett has stated that 90 percent of the products his company delivers on the final day of each year did not

Figure 1.1   Median Lifetime Earnings by Highest Educational Attainment, 2009 Dollars

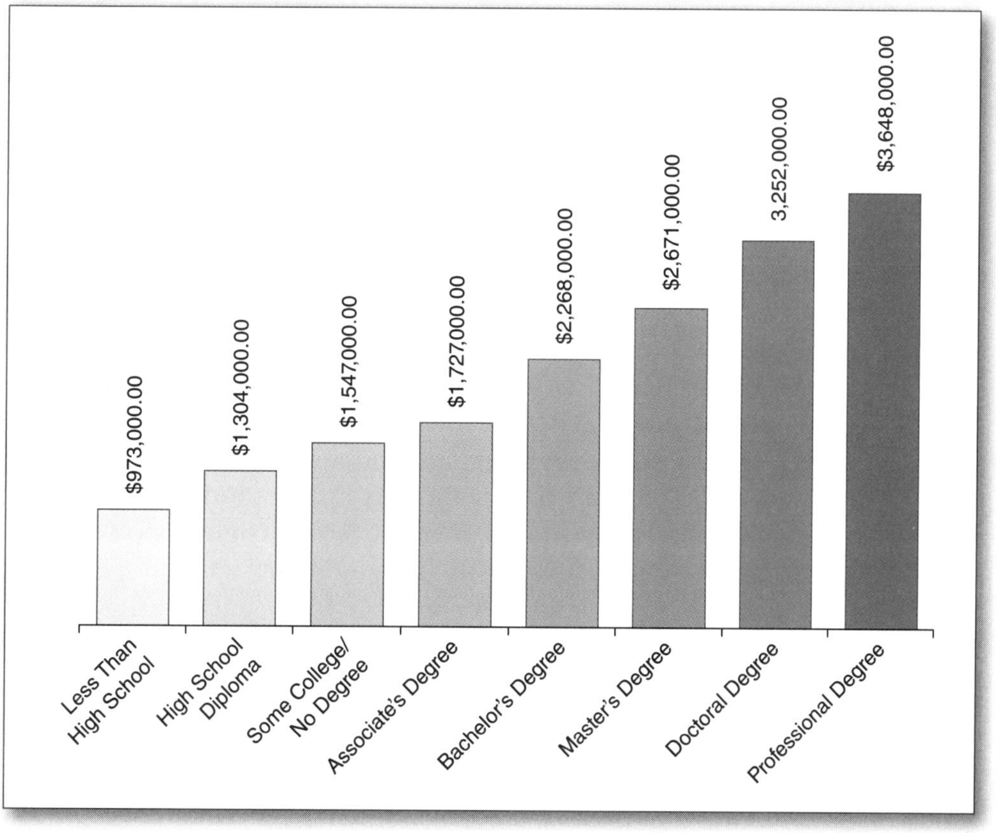

Source: Carnevale, A., Rose, S., & Cheah, B. (2011).

exist on the first day of the same year. To succeed in that kind of marketplace, U.S. firms need employees who are flexible, knowledgeable, and scientifically and mathematically literate (National Leadership Council for Liberal Education and America's Promise, 2007). The challenge for U.S. education, at all levels, is to prepare students to be able to keep up with this frenetic and unpredictable world and economy, in addition to sustaining the education of students who receive solid training in liberal arts fields. In the words of Andreas Schleicher, the Organisation for Economic Co-operation and Development (OECD) Education Directorate, "Schools have to prepare students for jobs that have not yet been created, technologies that have not yet been invented and problems that we don't know will arise" (2010). This is often a critical challenge for localities and regions—to utilize notoriously unreliable labor market forecasting data to inform the development of curricular pathways and school/postsecondary-based applied learning opportunities (see Chapter 4 for additional discussion).

The Need for Collaboration at All Levels

To provide the vast majority of high school students with the academic and nonacademic knowledge and skills they will need to succeed after high school, there will have to be unprecedented levels of collaboration between high schools and colleges and between the bodies that govern them. Historically, public education and higher education systems have operated independently. Until recently, high school teachers and college faculty rarely discussed jointly their expectations for students in their classes. High school counselors rarely met with college counselors to talk about whether they were helping their students prepare well for college. State boards of education, working in tandem with state educational agencies, adopted their own standards and accountability systems with little involvement from higher education. High schools focused on meeting state accountability requirements and on preparing an elite group of students to be eligible for admission to selective colleges—not for students to be ready to succeed in a wide variety of postsecondary educational settings, such as community colleges, apprenticeships, or training programs. Institutions of higher education (either as part of a state system or independently) determine admissions policies, courses,

> Until recently, high school teachers and college faculty rarely discussed jointly their expectations for students in their classes.

and curriculum, with wide variance in requirements, expectations, and alignment with workforce needs.

These disconnects have had serious ramifications for students—especially for students with the fewest educational and economic resources available through their families and communities (Venezia et al., 2003). High school curricula have traditionally been developed without consulting with postsecondary education, leading toward current disjunctures, such as different conceptions of writing and of algebra across the systems. Similarly, assessments have historically been disconnected, with entering college students often taking course placement tests that assess different knowledge and skills than were taught in their senior year—often with no warning and no ability to prepare. Students with familial, peer, and financial resources tend to weather these disconnects more successfully than do students without those benefits, due to such factors as supplemental supports and information from family or community members who have had experience with college and/or desired career paths.

The United States has historically focused solely on access to postsecondary education and training, rather than having a connected goal of postsecondary success, driven by a host of policy changes starting with the GI Bill in the 1940s, gaining steam in the 1960s with Lyndon B. Johnson's Great Society reforms, and a plethora of precollege outreach programs. In the past 10 years or so, faced with data showing that a large proportion of traditionally underserved students drop out of high school and college, educators, community leaders, and policymakers have concluded that the country has moved the needle on access, but that is not sufficient to provide excellent educational opportunities for a large number of students. Students need access to post-high school readiness—to ways to succeed in whatever they choose to pursue. That is a complex and highly personalized endeavor that will require new resources, relationships, and perspectives about the purpose and aims of education at all levels.

Many state and national efforts over the past decade have begun to address these disconnects between what high schools demand of students and what postsecondary institutions expect a mere three months later (for students who go directly from high school to college). In the field, these are called systems alignment issues. One state-level example is work being done in Texas. Beginning in 2007, the Texas Legislature passed legislation requiring the Texas Education Agency and the Texas Higher Education Coordinating Board to collaborate to support the Texas College and Career Readiness Initiative. This multiyear initiative has resulted in the creation of the Texas College and

Career Readiness Standards (TCCRS), jointly developed by vertical teams of secondary and postsecondary faculty members. Additional state-level work to support the initiative included incorporation of the TCCRS into the Texas Essential Knowledge and Skills and K–12 assessment system and the development of implementation materials to assist educators statewide in translating the TCCRS into practice.

At the national level, the largest effort to improve college and career readiness is represented by the Common Core. In June 2010, the Council of Chief State School Officers (CCSSO) and the National Governors Association Center for Best Practices (NGA Center) released the Common Core. The aim of the Common Core is to define the knowledge and skills students should achieve in order to graduate from high school ready to succeed in entry-level, credit-bearing college courses and in workforce training programs (CCSSO & NGA, 2011). The Common Core provides information about what students are expected to learn, no matter where they live. It is intended to be more rigorous than many states' current standards and to be more applied (Van Roekel, 2013). To date, 43 states, the District of Columbia, four territories, and the Department of Defense Education Activity have voluntarily adopted these national standards. Objectives of the Common Core are for states to have shared targets for both secondary and postsecondary systems to aim toward, and to collaborate across, state lines in the development and identification of best practices in curriculum, instruction, and assessments, while retaining flexibility on how to teach locally.

While a goal of the Common Core is to help close the gap between high schools and colleges, the standards have significant limitations. First, the Common Core only identifies the math and literacy skills students need to be successful beyond high school. This does not represent the complete set of knowledge and skills necessary for postsecondary readiness. Increasingly, educators and researchers are coming to an understanding that student success throughout K–12 and postsecondary education relies a great deal on key cognitive strategies, or habits of mind, such as persistence, resiliency, self-efficacy, organizational skills, communication skills, and so forth (see, e.g., Casner-Lotto & Benner, 2006; Conley, 2013). Some of these strategies can be developed and enhanced through experiences such as music, the arts, and contextual or applied learning opportunities. Second, the Common Core standards are not geared toward English Language Learners or students with special needs.

The Common Core is currently facing intense political scrutiny in states across the country. As summarized in *The Washington Post*, those on the right tend to view the Common Core as a federal intrusion toward a national curriculum interfering with state and local control.

Those on the left have voiced a number of issues surrounding the standards, including not enough input from educators into the drafting, that the standards are not based on any research, and that they ignore what is known about early childhood education (Strauss, 2013). In addition, there is concern across the political spectrum about the connection between adopting the Common Core and state applications for federal funding and the use of data from Common Core-aligned assessments for high stakes teacher evaluations.

The authors of this book are neither staunch supporters nor critics of the Common Core, although they use a critical lens to analyze new reform efforts. They are researchers and educators interested in furthering the identification and examination of the quality, implications, and impact of college and career readiness standards efforts. It is clear from our country's experimentation with standards since the 1990s that standards alone are not sufficient to change educational opportunities for our nation's underserved youth. A significant aspect of the Common Core, along with other states' college and career readiness standards (such as Alaska, Minnesota, Texas, and Virginia), in relation to this book, is that they provide a shared point of reference for high schools and colleges to work together. Faculty members and administrators can partner to examine the standards in relation to their current practice, and through this partnership, they can clearly articulate at the local level what knowledge and skills students need to be successful in that community. However, if these reference points are not appropriate, or if they are interpreted or implemented poorly, they can do more harm than good. This raises the most important issue: implementation—translating the vision of the Common Core into classroom-based practice—is the biggest challenge for the Common Core initiative. Providing enough support and resources for teachers and administrators to change current practice is critically important.

Blame the System

The question, "What did we do wrong?" from the family at the Northern California community college reveals a major challenge in engaging in communitywide efforts to improve college and career readiness. These conversations, if not carefully framed, can quickly devolve into finger-pointing and focusing on blame, not solutions.

> What needs to be emphasized throughout the process is that this is a systems alignment issue; no group or institution is solely responsible for creating the problems, and no one group or educational entity can solve the problems individually.

What needs to be emphasized throughout the process is that this is a systems alignment issue; no group or institution is solely responsible for creating the problems, and no one group or educational entity can solve the problems individually. In one poignant editorial being circulated on the Internet, a recently retired high school teacher, Kenneth Bernstein, issued a warning to college professors:

> No Child Left Behind went into effect for the 2002–03 academic year, which means that America's public schools have been operating under the pressures and constrictions imposed by that law for a decade. . . . Please do not blame those of us in public schools for how unprepared for higher education the students arriving at your institutions are. We have very little say in what is happening to public education. Even the most distinguished and honored among us have trouble getting our voices heard in the discussion about educational policy. (Bernstein, 2013)

Teachers and schools work very hard to educate their students well. Students and families work hard to meet the high school graduation and college admissions requirements. Education and workforce systems have worked largely in isolation in setting standards, expectations, and requirements. There have been no mutually agreed upon targets for student readiness post-high school; in fact, each postsecondary institution creates its own entry-level expectations (and many individual faculty members do as well within their own classrooms). While this is an important hallmark of academic freedom, it also makes it incredibly challenging to signal to students—particularly traditionally underrepresented students who would be the first in their families to go to college—the key knowledge and skills they need to be successful after they graduate from high school. In short, everyone has been working very hard to do exactly what the different systems have been holding them accountable to do, driven by their own passions to do right by students.

The critical messaging to avoid the "blame game" is to keep the focus on the need for shared responsibility to move forward. All community members share this challenge—students, educators, families, community leaders, employers, and more—to build successful educational pathways that span from early childhood to adulthood. Whereas state and national efforts are beginning to address these system misalignment issues, true change occurs at the local level. The existence of a state or national framework to support high school and college partnerships can help prod the work toward common goals and objectives, but ultimately, collaborations of local educators, workforce representatives, and community representatives drive the reform efforts enabling students to be prepared for success beyond high school in that locality. Communities need not wait for state or federal direction; they can and do engage in this critical work independently. By moving beyond fault finding and instead toward emphasizing the need for shared responsibility, the conversations can be shaped constructively to pave the way for student and community success.

The remainder of this book outlines how a community can come together to overcome the historically disconnected educational systems. Whereas federal and state support can provide valuable resources and assistance in expediting such efforts, this is not a necessary element. Local stakeholders can do this work with or without external support. What is necessary is a shared vision that every student in the community should graduate high school ready to succeed. This book details how to accomplish this critical endeavor.

SUMMARY

College and career readiness share many important elements, including core knowledge and skills from across the curriculum, study skills, time-management skills, persistence, ownership of learning, problem solving, collecting and analyzing information, and communicating in a variety of ways. The intersection and overlap between what students need to know and be able to do to be ready for college and for entering a career represent what all students need when they graduate high school. The outlying areas represent the knowledge and skills that are unique to their specific postsecondary and career fields. College and career readiness, then, represent the intersection: the knowledge, skills, and abilities that all students need to make the next step, without remediation, along their desired career pathway. This conception has evolved from a focus on access to postsecondary education to a focus on success in college and career preparation, and it requires the need to collaborate at all levels and not assert blame on a particular part of our educational system.

DISCUSSION QUESTIONS

- Do you agree with the authors' definition of college and career readiness? Why or why not? What could be an alternative definition?
- Should all students have the opportunity to become prepared for some form of postsecondary education?

- When should college and career readiness activities start, ideally? How can those activities be scaffolded for students and faculty over time?
- Given the wide range of postsecondary options, how can all high schools provide students with high quality readiness opportunities— both academic and applied?
- Should applied postsecondary readiness activities also have an integrated academic core? What are the pros and cons of such an approach?

Creating a Framework

Isolated college and career-related activities are routine in most American high schools. Often, these activities are disconnected from college-level expectations, and many lack applied components, such as work-based learning opportunities. Events such as college fairs, providing outside speakers from different occupations, college sweatshirt or T-shirt day, internship opportunities, and test preparation for college admission tests are common. Most high schools and institutions of higher education in America have some established relationships and joint activities. For example, a survey of matriculation officers from California's community colleges reported that respondents said they engaged in the following activities to reach high school students: visited high schools more than once a year (83 percent), met with high school counselors and/or teachers to discuss college readiness or preparation issues (91 percent), brought high school students to the college campus to learn about assessment and placement requirements (87 percent), and conducted placement testing at the high school campuses (84 percent; Venezia, Bracco, & Nodine, 2010). This situation is likely similar in states across the country, yet college remediation rates remain high. The differences between most existing efforts and the partnership model envisioned here are the focus, comprehensiveness, and mutual coordination of these efforts.

A key distinguishing feature of the partnership model described in this book is the comprehensiveness of the initiative. Throughout the United States, local communities are working in earnest to support high school students. These efforts, however, are typically episodic and piecemeal with little coordination or shared focus. As an example, in 2011, McGaughy conducted a workshop supported by the Office of Public Instruction in the state of Washington. The audience for the workshop consisted of leadership teams representing seven regional partnerships in the third year of an initiative to help students make clear, careful, and creative choices for college and career. During the course of the workshop, a prominent theme emerged. All of the partnerships had planned and executed events and activities related to college and career readiness, but in the third year, they felt their efforts beginning to stall in creating new ideas to implement. What they were missing was a framework to guide their work. As one participating superintendent commented, "Before we were coming up with neat ideas that sounded good to us; now we have a map to guide our future planning."

The map, or conceptual framework, used to drive the partnership model described in this book is the Four Keys to College and Career Readiness (the Four Keys), developed by David Conley when he was CEO of EPIC. The Four Keys describe what students need to be fully prepared to succeed in postsecondary learning settings aligned to their aspirations and help educators organize instruction and supports to prepare all students for college and career readiness. Research provides insight into the limitations of traditional standards and assessments. College faculty report that while students often lack sufficient content knowledge in their fields of study, a more significant problem is their inability to apply their knowledge (Conley, 2010). Numerous studies point to a similar need for aspiring career professionals in the 21st-century occupational environments to have general skills such as flexible and critical thinking, problem solving, creativity, and communication, along with the ability to collaborate in multifunctional and diverse teams (Casner-Lotto & Benner, 2006; Kuther, 2013).

> The Four Keys describe what students need to be fully prepared to succeed in postsecondary learning settings aligned to their aspirations and help educators organize instruction and supports to prepare all students for college and career readiness.

According to Conley (2005), school curriculum often tends to focus on declarative learning (repeating facts) and procedural learning (following directions), instead of on conceptual learning. Content-based assessments do not necessarily gauge the cognitive capabilities and strategies that students are expected to demonstrate in entry-level college courses and beyond.

Further, research suggests that to be prepared for college and career success, students must have a variety of knowledge, skills, and abilities. EPIC has conducted multiple analyses of entry-level courses required for the range of postsecondary options, including career certificates as well as associate and bachelor degrees (Conley, 2005; Conley, McGaughy, Brown, van der Valk, & Young, 2009; Conley et al., 2009; Conley, Drummond, de Gonzalez, Rooseboom, & Stout, 2011a). These results suggest that although there are differences between college readiness and career readiness, they share important elements, including a range of cognitive strategies, study skills, time management, persistence, and ownership of learning. The Four Keys (see Figure 2.1) are grounded in this research.

The Four Keys can be most easily remembered as Think, Know, Act, and Go (For a complete description of the Four Keys and the supporting research, please refer to Conley, 2013.):

Key Cognitive Strategies (KCS, also referred to as Think): This key describes the ways of thinking necessary for postsecondary work. It enables students and workers to address problems independently

Figure 2.1 The Four Keys to College and Career Readiness

Key Cognitive Strategies	Key Content Knowledge	Key Learning Skills and Techniques	Key Transition Knowledge and Skills
Think	Know	Act	Go
Problem Formulation Hypothesize Strategize **Research** Identify Collect **Interpretation** Analyze Evaluate **Communication** Organize Construct **Precision and Accuracy** Monitor Confirm	**Structure of Knowledge** Key Terms and Terminology Factual Information Linking Ideas Organizing Concepts **Attitudes Toward Learning Content** Challenge Level Value Attribution Effort **Technical Knowledge and Skills** Specific College and Career Readiness Standards	**Ownership of Learning** Goal Setting Persistence Self-Awareness Motivation Help-Seeking Progress Monitoring Self-Efficacy **Learning Techniques** Time Management Test-Taking Skills Note-Taking Skills Memorization/Recall Strategic Reading Collaborative Learning Technology	**Contextual** Aspirations Norms/Culture **Procedural** Institution Choice Admission Process **Financial** Tuition Financial Aid **Cultural** Postsecondary Norms **Personal** Self-Advocacy Institutional Context

Source: Conley, D. (2013).

and apply their content knowledge in unique, nonroutine, and novel situations. This key includes five components that result in a cycle of inquiry: problem formulation, research, interpretation, communication, and precision/accuracy. Examples of what this looks like in practice include the following:

- The KCS can be found embedded throughout recent college and career readiness standards, including the Cross-Disciplinary Standards of the Texas College and Career Readiness Standards (www.thecb.state.tx.us/collegereadiness/crs.pdf) and Standards for Mathematical Practice in the Common Core State Standards (www.corestandards.org/Math/Practice).
- In CTE, the KCS are commonly used when teaching students to apply their knowledge and skills. For example, the National Research Center for Career and Technical Education has developed curriculum integration models that embody a contextualized approach to integrate CTE content into rigorous and authentic applications in career pathways (see www.nrccte .org/core-issues/curriculum-integration).

Key Content Knowledge (KCK, also referred to as Know): This key describes the foundational content and big ideas from the subject areas necessary for students to achieve their aspirations. Also included in this key are the technical knowledge and skills associated with specific career aspirations, the ways in which students interact with content knowledge, its perceived value to them, the effort they are willing to expend to learn necessary content, and their belief about why they succeed or fail in mastering this knowledge. Examples of what this looks like in practice include the following:

- EPIC completed a national study, titled *Reaching the Goal*, on the Common Core, to consider what specific literacy and math skills are necessary for postsecondary readiness. A national sample of postsecondary instructors who teach entry-level general education and CTE courses were asked to rate the applicability and importance of each standard for their courses. The results list what specific standards are applicable and the level of importance in 25 entry-level courses (Conley et al., 2011a).
- For technical standards, the National Association of State Directors of Career Technical Education Consortium coordinated the development of the Common Career Technical Core (CCTC). The CCTC includes sets of standards for each of the

16 career clusters and their corresponding career pathways that define what students should know and be able to do after completing instruction in a program of study (www.careertech .org/CCTC).

Key Learning Skills and Techniques (KLST, also referred to as Act): This key describes the beliefs, behaviors, and strategies students must have to succeed in formal learning environments, including the workforce. This key consists of two categories:

- *Student ownership of learning,* which includes goal setting, persistence, self-awareness, motivation, help-seeking, progress monitoring, and self-efficacy.
- *Specific learning techniques and strategies,* such as time management, test-taking and note-taking skills, memorization/recall, strategic reading, collaborative learning, and technology.

The KLST, including skills often referred to as "soft skills," are needed to succeed in most academic and professional settings. Examples of what this looks like in practice include the following:

- Teachers from nine school districts in the San Antonio, Texas, region worked with EPIC to develop a database, called SA Ready, of lesson plans from Grades K–12, aligned to the Four Keys. Available for free, the database can be searched by tags related to the KLST, including persistence, motivation, goals, self-monitoring, study skills, organization, and note taking. These lesson plans offer concrete examples of how to teach these skills across grades and subject areas (www.SA-Ready.org).
- The Office of Disability Employment Policy (ODEP) has created a curriculum, titled, "Skills to Pay the Bills—Mastering Soft Skills for Workplace Success" (www.dol.gov/odep/topics/ youth/softskills). Created for youth ages 14–21, this program is comprised of modular, hands-on activities to build interpersonal and professional skills for the workplace.

Key Transition Knowledge and Skills (KTKS, also referred to as Go): This key describes the procedural and contextual knowledge and skills students need to navigate to achieve their aspirations. This information has often been privileged knowledge and not equally accessible to all students. The least likely students to possess this information are those from families and communities historically underrepresented in higher education or certain career pathways. This key includes the contextual, procedural, financial, cultural, and personal aspects related to successfully navigating a desired career path. Examples of what this looks like in practice include the following:

- The Roadtrip Nation Experience (roadtripnation.org) is a project-based, self-discovery curriculum that enables students to explore the contextual and personal dimensions of their transition to life after high school. The program has students map their interest to future pathways, explore their communities, and speak with local leaders to learn the steps they took to get where they are.
- Federal Student Aid, an Office of the U.S. Department of Education, offers support for students and parents with federal financial aid checklists, resources, and steps available for elementary, middle, high school, and adult students (studentaid .ed.gov/prepare-for-college/checklists#checklists).

The Four Keys were selected as the conceptual framework to guide the partnership model for multiple reasons. First, as described throughout this chapter, the framework was developed based on extensive research from entry-level general education and CTE instructors and coursework. Second, it is a comprehensive framework that provides a practical organization of "think, know, act, go" for a complex myriad of knowledge, skills, and abilities necessary for postsecondary readiness. Third, the Four Keys have been used around the country since 2006 to guide many initiatives and efforts to improve college and career readiness. This body of work provides an extensive amount of tools and lessons learned from the field that are the basis of this book.

Most importantly, however, the Four Keys are a powerful tool for organizing college and career readiness partnerships. They represent a new pair of glasses that clearly focuses the purpose of the partnership and a map to guide the direction of the work that needs to be undertaken. The Four Keys serve as the foundation of the remainder of the book. They should be used to help create the vision and select the goals and objectives as described in Chapter 3. They should then be used as a reference point to determine the outcomes and indicators used in measuring the success of the partnership work as detailed in Chapter 4. Finally, as described in Chapter 5, the Four Keys should be used as the framework to map and plan what strategies, activities, and programming the partnership should support. A critical element that must not be overlooked is that the Four Keys are for all students, not just students who enter high school academically prepared. In the words of Allen and Murphy (2008), "Rather than target the subset of students who are on track to graduation and college, postsecondary partnerships must be deep and broad enough to affect all students in a school" (p. 4). The Four Keys represent how a partnership knows if it is taking a comprehensive approach to improving college and career readiness as long as all Four Keys are being developed in all students.

> The Four Keys are a powerful tool for organizing college and career readiness partnerships. They represent a new pair of glasses that clearly focuses the purpose of the partnership and a map to guide the direction of the work that needs to be undertaken.

SUMMARY

Many ad hoc activities exist to help high school students prepare for life after graduation. The differences between most existing efforts and the partnership model envisioned in this book are the focus, comprehensiveness, and mutual coordination of this work. The framework for this book and the suggested framework for partnerships is the Four Keys to College and Career Readiness (Conley, 2013): Think (key cognitive strategies, such as effective problem formulation), Know (key content knowledge, both academic and applied), Act (key learning skills and techniques such as student ownership of learning and soft skills), and Go (key transition knowledge and techniques, such as necessary financial aid information).

DISCUSSION QUESTIONS

- Do you think that the Four Keys include all of the necessary components to help a larger proportion of students be prepared to succeed after high school? If not, what is missing?
- When you compare your school's or partnership's current efforts to the Four Keys model, what is missing in your work?

Organizing the
Partnership

L ocal partnerships focused on supporting or improving education
are common. The difference between traditional partnerships and
the partnership model envisioned here is a comprehensive focus on
postsecondary readiness and success, though they are not mutually
exclusive. For example, many partnerships focus on supporting social–
emotional and physical health for students and their families; keeping
that focus and adding an emphasis on postsecondary readiness and
success could be a powerful combination. The typical educational
reform approach of adopting discrete "best practices" and trying to
bring them to scale will not work; what is needed is a "best process"
approach to create a systemic, integrated, and connected student success pathway or set of pathways for all students, touching on both the
academic and nonacademic facets of their lives (O'Banion, 2011).

The potential benefits of partnering are manifold. Research has
found that "although partnership work is challenging, and more
partnerships fail than succeed, successful partnerships can achieve
goals that individual agencies cannot" (Wildridge, Childs, Cawthra,
& Madge, 2004, p. 4). Involving more people, perspectives, and institutional resources in a partnership can result in the following: (a) an
increased capacity and expanded ability to do the work, along with

improved quality of solutions; (b) improved relationships among the different partnering entities; (c) aligned services, more closely meeting students' and their families' needs; (d) better use of resources; (e) a more creative approach to problems; and (f) an increase in influence on others (Wildridge et al., 2004). Partnerships allow for a collaborative advantage, enabling a community to achieve what would be impossible for an individual institution to accomplish working in isolation.

A challenge is that there is no cookie-cutter approach to building successful partnerships. The question of where to start depends on myriad factors, such as the status of preexisting relationships, leadership, resources, needs of different student groups in the community, and the history of civic engagement and reform efforts in the community (Wildridge et al., 2004). No one currently knows how many local partnerships exist or have previously existed in the United States. In the 1990s, the now defunct National Association for Partnerships in Education (NAPE) conducted extensive polling and estimated that there were roughly 144,000 school and business partnerships in the country (Rochford, 2007). These numerous efforts have great variance in scope, purpose, participation, and effectiveness. Few rigorous evaluations of partnership programs have taken place (Barnett et al., 2012). Given the lack of information available about partnerships and the importance of context in driving the goals, objectives, frameworks, processes, composition, and so forth, it is impossible to write a how-to manual with precise steps.

> Partnerships allow for a collaborative advantage, enabling a community to achieve what would be impossible for an individual institution to accomplish working in isolation.

To begin, each community must build partnerships based on its own context. Instead of a one-size-fits-all prescriptive task list of how to build a strong partnership, this book recommends that each partnership embrace "possibility thinking." This approach asks participants to move beyond history, deficits, blame, and limitations to focus on what genuinely can be possible (Rochford, 2007). This includes leveraging existing relationships and resources and building off of activities and programs already in place to create a comprehensive initiative addressing all Four Keys to College and Career Readiness. The remainder of this chapter explores the process of starting or expanding local partnerships to improve college and career readiness. This includes establishing leadership, developing a vision, selecting an organizing structure or model, and creating a college and career readiness culture.

Area 1: Establishing Leadership

The first step in establishing a college and career readiness partnership is to secure leadership to direct the work. For a partnership to succeed, it must have the leadership and organizational capacity to engage members in needed work tasks to produce the desired outcomes. This capacity, at any level, requires a strong leadership base, with leaders "who have the skills (e.g., communication, conflict resolution, resource development, and administration), relationships (e.g., internal and external), and vision to transform individual interests into a dynamic collective force that achieves targeted outcomes" (Foster-Fishman, Berkowitz, Lounsbury, Jacobson, & Allen, 2001, p. 243).

> For a partnership to succeed, it must have the leadership and organizational capacity to engage members in needed work tasks to produce the desired outcomes.

The leadership to launch the partnership should be thought of at two levels. First, high level leadership is needed that has decision-making and resource allocation authority to prioritize the work. In a comprehensive initiative such as this, the higher the authority of the leaders driving the work, the greater the potential to make systemic changes. At the beginning, leaders from a college or university and from the local school districts need to be involved. Eventually, leaders representing all of the major educational institutions (such as universities, community colleges, and feeder school districts) and community organizations (such as parent organizations, teacher unions, and community service providers), along with business representatives from the major economic sectors in the community, should participate. Ideally, at the local level, the leaders will authorize staff to conduct the work, provide thought leadership, and prioritize resources and support (including the recruitment of advocates) for these vital efforts.

The second level of leadership that needs to occur is the facilitation of the actual work. These are the implementers of what the executive leaders decide needs to be done in the community to produce desired outcomes. They have the authority from their CEOs to run the partnership and, importantly, the CEOs stay briefed on key partnership activities and can jump in when necessary. These "second level" individuals can be thought of as "boundary scanners." They have skills in working across professional, organizational, or other boundaries (Wildridge et al., 2004). The historical architecture of education encourages "silos," not collaboration, and requires individuals who can bridge these institutional divides both internally and externally. For example, in higher education, faculty members divide into departments around disciplines; staff members in student affairs and academic affairs hardly communicate on some campuses; and curriculum is halved into career/technical education and liberal arts/transfer education (O'Banion, 2011). These boundary scanners are often deans (such as for Instruction, Academic Affairs, Student Affairs, and College of Education), assistant superintendents (particularly overseeing curriculum and instruction, assessment, and counseling), department chairs (such as for mathematics, English/language arts, and CTE), human resource managers of businesses, and program directors at community organizations.

Practically, this all starts with a convener. Someone in the community must step forward or be appointed to begin the conversation with as many of the institutional leaders as possible. One approach is to have an intermediary organization facilitate the work, such as a local nonprofit organization or educational service center. Another approach is to have educational institutions dedicate FTE to staff the work, or there can be a combination of the two; often the "backbone" work of the partnerships needs to be provided by multiple entities. This could be accomplished by appointing co-conveners, such as a representative from the college and one from a school district, to recruit participants, plan agendas, send out invitations, facilitate the meetings, and coordinate action steps. It is critically important for the facilitator to be well-respected by all of the entities involved in the partnership. The partnership can live or die largely based on the facilitator's abilities and standing in the community.

For recruiting partnership representatives, Chapter 1 of this book can be used to guide those conversations, providing the rationale to obtain buy-in from the key players to improve college and career readiness. An important issue to remember is the philosophy behind this partnership work. Engage in "possibility thinking"—focus on what can be achieved and not on blame, barriers, and limitations. If some of the necessary stakeholders are not ready to participate, start with those who are, but be aware of the possible ramifications of starting without key partners. This process is a continuum building on

> The National Taskforce on Community Leadership developed a framework for community foundations to take a leadership role in partnership development. The framework can be accessed here: http://www.cfleads.org/resources/commleadership_pubs/docs/CF_framewrk_OV_120408.pdf.

what exists and expanding on what is doable. Even a partnership at the smallest level, consisting of two instructors, one at the college level and one at the high school level, can bring individuals together to align their curricula so that their students are prepared to make a successful transition in their courses. They can then share their success with colleagues, build an evidence base, and foster interest and support in growing this partnership work.

> Engage in "possibility thinking"—focus on what can be achieved and not on blame, barriers, and limitations.

A challenging aspect of the leadership development is that there can be a clash of cultures between educators and business representatives. K–12 and postsecondary educators are used to faculty governance models that, while collaborative, are often not expeditious. Business leaders, on the other hand, tend to make decisions quickly, need many weeks in advance to schedule meetings, and have high financial opportunity costs with regard to the time spent in meetings. Local leaders must be aware of these differences and work together to bridge the cultures.

Strategies for Establishing Leadership

Who should be involved?

Executive Leadership Team:

- Chancellors or presidents of local two- and four-year colleges and universities
- Superintendents of local school districts
- Local elected officials (such as state legislators and board members)
- Presidents of local community organizations (such as parent-teacher, teacher unions, and human service providers)
- Business representatives from the major economic sectors in the community

Vertical Teams (organized by discipline or areas of focus):

- College deans (such as for Instruction, Academic Affairs, Student Affairs, and College of Education)
- Assistant superintendents (particularly overseeing curriculum and instruction, assessment, and counseling)
- Department chairs from both local colleges and high schools (such as for mathematics, English/language arts, and CTE)
- Training managers from local businesses
- Program directors at community organizations

Talking points for recruitment:

- A high school diploma does not offer the same opportunities it used to. We live in a certificate-based economy, meaning most professions, particularly those offering clear advancement opportunities, require some formal training beyond high school.
- Current high school graduation requirements do not align with what students need to be successful beyond high school. There are preparations gaps for a wide variety of postsecondary options, such as college, job training programs, apprenticeships, and military service.
- College and career readiness means high school graduates have the knowledge and skills necessary to successfully transition to the next step in their desired career pathway, without remediation.
- Remediation is a serious problem: Nationally, around 60 percent of students entering community colleges require at least one remedial or developmental education course (Note: Mention the percentage of students requiring remediation at the local community college if available). Remedial education is costly—students pay for the courses but do not receive college credit, so it takes extra time and money to finish college.
- Historically, secondary and postsecondary educational systems have operated independently, creating gaps and misalignment between the two systems.
- Locally driven action has the power to improve college and career readiness for all students. By moving beyond fault finding and instead toward emphasizing the need for shared responsibility, local educators, workforce representatives, and community representatives can drive the reform efforts necessary to enable students to be prepared for success beyond high school in that community.

The "ask":

Executive Leadership Team:

"For the partnership to succeed, your voice and perspective must be part of the process. Please attend the kick-off meeting, and come prepared to share your expertise in supporting this critical effort."

Vertical Teams:

"We must partner to close the gaps created by the separate high school and college systems. We have the power locally to close those gaps. You have been selected because of your deep expertise in [the area being addressed by the vertical team, such as mathematics or counseling]. Please attend the kick-off meeting for your vertical team, and come prepared to share your expertise in making our students successful beyond high school."

Area 2: Developing a Vision

Creating a shared vision is the linchpin for buy-in, support, and coordination of efforts. The vision expresses what the partnership will achieve and how it will be achieved. It expresses the "what" or the end goal and is often paired with a mission statement that is the "how to" or the actions that will be taken to achieve the vision. Without a common, agreed on vision, everyone "is left to his or her own devices to imagine one—a scenario that results in unharnessed and unfocused efforts, with everyone believing that what he or she is doing is right" (Gabriel & Farmer, 2009). Nanus (1992) identified five characteristics for an effective vision statement:

1. Attracts commitment and energizes people.

2. Creates meaning in people's lives.

3. Establishes a standard of excellence.

4. Bridges the present to the future.

5. Transcends the status quo.

Getting the executive leadership team to agree on a shared vision guides the future work. A shared vision provides a clear target to refer to when making decisions about the important work to be done to achieve the vision. It must be actionable.

Creating a shared vision for the postsecondary partnership should be the primary objective for the initial kick-off meeting for the executive leadership team. A facilitator should lead the partnership members through an activity to draft a vision. One engaging activity developed by EPIC researchers for use with educational stakeholders in reaching group consensus to develop a vision is based on design charette strategies. (For an example of EPIC's work using this approach, please see Collins, Davis-Molin, McGaughy, & Conley, 2013.) Borrowed from the planning and design fields, a design charette is an intensely focused session intended to foster creativity and build consensus among participants, develop specific goals and solutions, and motivate stakeholders to be committed to reaching the collaboratively developed goals (Lindsey, Todd, & Hayter, 2009). This particular activity, termed

> Creating a shared vision for the postsecondary partnership should be the primary objective for the initial kick-off meeting for the executive leadership team.

"True North," asks the leadership team members to work together to develop the vision and goals to guide the partnership work.

The multiple-step activity begins by reviewing definitions of college and career readiness, such as the one presented in the first chapter of this book. Participants are then asked to discuss with a neighbor their personal vision of what knowledge and skills students need to be college and career ready when they leave high school to be successful in their community. To capture individual responses, one partner writes on an index card while the other partner speaks, and then after five minutes, the roles are reversed. Each group of partners then shares its results with the whole group. A facilitator then captures the responses for all to see. The entire group then works together to organize the responses into similar sized categories, ultimately generating a list of the knowledge and skills that were identified by the partnership discussions.

For the second part of the activity, each stakeholder receives three voting dots (stickers) to "vote" for his or her top three priorities to be included in the group's vision of what a college and career ready student in their community should be. When voting is finished, the group can then visually see the priorities and use the top categories as the foundation for writing its vision statement and developing its goals. The group then solicits one or more volunteer to draft the vision and mission statement based on the True North results. The draft language is then emailed to participants to review and provide feedback before being finalized at the next meeting.

Sample Vision Statement and Goals

For example, partners in Imperial County, California, developed the following vision statement and goals to increase postsecondary readiness (Imperial County Office of Education, n.d.).

Vision

The Imperial Valley P-16 Council is a preschool through higher education community collaborative promoting a college-going culture. The Council's vision is to increase significantly student eligibility, admittance, and attendance at post-secondary institutions.

(Continued)

> (Continued)
>
> ## Goals
>
> 1. To support the achievement of rigorous coursework in mathematics, English, including writing, and science for all students.
>
> 2. To provide information, resources, and opportunities for students and their families to increase expectations and develop enthusiasm about college as a viable option.
>
> 3. To increase community-wide knowledge about the P-16 Council and the support of the Imperial County College-Going Initiative and enlist fiscal resources for its accomplishment.
>
> 4. To develop and implement strategies to assess and address obstacles to college completion in Imperial County for local students, including transfers from community college. (p. 1)

Area 3: Selecting an Organizing Structure or Model

The next step is determining the desired organizing structure for operating the partnership. Rochford (2007) developed a typography of local and regional efforts, ranging on a continuum from a partnership involving a single college and school district focusing on one single program, to a partnership involving multiple school districts, institutions of higher education, and community organizations, with long-term strategies and multiple programs. Where a partnership is on the continuum is determined by the community leadership willing to participate and the agreed on outcomes, coupled with the strength of existing relationships and programming. These partnerships should intentionally focus on process and moving through the continuum in stages to promote a genuine culture change, resulting in changed mind-sets and practices. To truly achieve the systemic change necessary to improve college and career readiness, the partnerships need to ultimately involve all of the major stakeholders in the community. Through partnerships, "community leaders think together, even dream together, about what can be. It is the building of civic capacity" (Rochford, 2007, p. 84).

As mentioned earlier, partnership work is ubiquitous around the country. Partnership efforts do not need to start from scratch. There are multiple examples of partnership models to improve college and career readiness that can be considered and customized to fit local needs and priorities, such as those connected to P–16/20 Partnerships, Early College High Schools, Project Lead the Way, National Career Clusters, Perkins, the National Association of State Directors of Career Technical Education Consortium, the Common Career Technical Core, Technology Centers that Work (through the Southern Regional Education Board), and Linked Learning in California. The following section describes three models, providing examples of a range of approaches for partnerships to consider what would work best for their local community:

P–16/20 Partnerships: This is an integrated system of education designed to raise student achievement at all levels, from preschool through a baccalaureate degree. The focus of these partnerships is on the interrelated nature of the education pipeline, an idea that goes as far back as the 1980s (Krueger, 2006). P–16/20 councils have been created in 40 states. These councils are intended to create a unified governance system from preschool through postsecondary education—well beyond the traditional focus on K–12 education that goes only through high school. In theory, these councils create a seamless transition between all grade levels, particularly between high school and college, by aligning standards and curriculum so students leave high school better prepared for postsecondary education (Weldon, 2009). P–16 approaches at the state level must be complemented by P–16 councils at the local or regional levels. These are the groups that "operationalize" any long-term P–16 approach (Rochford, 2007).

Early College High Schools: One integrated partnership model blends high school and college in a rigorous yet supportive program, compressing the time it takes to complete high school and the first two years of college. The schools are designed so that low-income youth, first-generation college goers, English Language Learners, students of color, and other young people underrepresented in higher education can simultaneously earn a high school diploma and one to two years of transferable college credit—tuition free (Allen & Murphy, 2008).

Alternative Governance Model: This approach would be a "do-it-yourself" option to tailor the organization to what works in a particular local context. One example at the state level is a mandatory joint strategic planning process, which could also be implemented at a local level. For example, in Ohio, House Bill 1 mandated that, "Not later than December 1, 2009, the superintendent of public instruction shall develop a ten-year strategic plan aligned with the strategic plan for higher education developed by the chancellor of the Ohio Board of

Regents" (Weldon, 2009, p. 6). Therefore, even without a formal P–16/20 council in place, Ohio law will require articulation between K–12 and postsecondary education (Weldon, 2009). The approach, the requirement of strategic planning, allows local communities to design their own planning process.

Area 4: Creating a College and Career Readiness Culture

Improving readiness to succeed after high school begins with understanding and support from educators and families. One of the key findings from a study of high schools that prepare a greater than expected proportion of students for college and career readiness is the existence of a strong college and career readiness culture (see, e.g., Conley, 2010; McDonough, 1997). Building this culture includes making success after high school an explicit communitywide goal, signaling to students through both symbolic and substantive ways that the goal of high school is to prepare students for success in adult life—in postsecondary education and in their workplaces. Adults in the community must demonstrate, repeatedly, that they expect all students to become college and career ready. If adults do not share this belief and believe that only some students should be ready, students can internalize this and see themselves as part of the group not destined to succeed. In short, the focus is on how to prepare for college and postsecondary learning, not whether or not to apply in the first place.

Again, college and career readiness do not mean setting the bar at matriculation into a four-year college or university. Creating the culture should entail working with students to set goals and plan for life after high school, while also allowing for flexibility so that students can explore their interests, since few teenagers know what they want to be when they grow up. The community must have high expectations for all students defined as participation in some form of postsecondary learning, whether to attend a college or pursue a career-oriented opportunity. This includes symbolic rituals such as billboards, pep rallies, and award ceremonies for postsecondary admissions, special programs such as summer bridge and orientation programs for first-year students, and policies that by default place students into rigorous courses and programs of study aligned to entry-level postsecondary courses (Conley, 2010). (Please refer to Chapter 5, "Category 1: Building a College and Career Readiness Culture," for explicit examples and activities for how to create a college and career readiness culture.)

Overall, improving college and career readiness is a communitywide endeavor that must be spearheaded by a leadership team of key local decision makers and supported by vertical teams of professionals empowered to do the work. This chapter addressed the process for how to formulate and operate a college and career readiness partnership. Such deep systemic change is a process, not a program. To be successful, this process must include a solid organizational structure and be driven by a culture with a pervasive belief that all students will graduate ready to succeed in some form of postsecondary education.

> The community must have high expectations for all students defined as participation in some form of postsecondary learning, whether to attend a college or pursue a career-oriented opportunity.

SUMMARY

Partnerships allow for a collaborative advantage, enabling a community to achieve what would be impossible for an individual school or postsecondary institution to accomplish working in isolation. The most challenging aspect of providing assistance to partnerships is that there is no one-size-fits-all model. Partnership models, goals, and objectives depend on such factors as the status of preexisting relationships, leadership, resources, needs of different student groups in the community, and the history of civic engagement and reform efforts in the community. The major steps involved in creating an effective partnership include establishing leadership, developing a vision, selecting a governance approach or model, and creating a college and career readiness culture.

DISCUSSION QUESTIONS

- Who are the key leaders in your community that need to be involved to create an effective partnership?
- Does your partnership have a "backbone" organization or set of organizations (that provides that infrastructure for the work) that is well-respected by all entities in the partnership?
- Is the leadership viewed as unbiased and effective?
- Is there a collective vision and set of goals and objectives that are aligned with the vision?
- Is there agreement within your partnership about the college and career readiness culture you are striving to create and maintain?

Determining Your Partnership's Effectiveness: Measuring Progress

After establishing a college and career readiness partnership with a vision and goals (as described in the previous chapter), how will the partnership's stakeholders know if the work is successful and making an impact toward achieving those goals? This chapter describes the next step in the process of building an effective partnership, which is to determine the biggest needs and then decide which outcomes and indicators will be measured to monitor success. The outcome measures should be tied directly to the goals, serving as the ultimate standards against which the end results of the partnership efforts should be assessed. For example, if one goal of the partnership is to increase the number of students obtaining a certificate, credential, or degree after high school, monitoring the change in those numbers should be the outcomes measured. The outcomes represent the end results. What also needs to be measured, but are typically more complex, are indicators that occur along the way. Indicators are interim measures that provide a signal for a later outcome. Effective indicators can be used to identify students on track, or not on track, to achieve outcomes. They also highlight actionable leverage points for impacting or altering the desired outcome (University of Chicago Consortium on Chicago School Research, 2014).

One of the big stumbling blocks to developing an effective P–16 partnership often centers on data use. Our schools and many of our postsecondary institutions were not designed to be hubs of data analysis, and their data are collected and used in isolation from each other. Educators are tasked with so many responsibilities, and deciding on indicators and developing data systems require specialized expertise. Over the years, more districts and postsecondary institutions have hired staff with quantitative expertise, but people with that skill set often are not immersed in the educational side of the house enough to determine which indicators should be used. To add another layer of difficulty, most educational data systems do not span across K–12 and postsecondary education, making it impossible to understand the effects of certain interventions in K–12 on postsecondary progress and completion. Given that there are available models and reinventing this wheel is time-consuming, this chapter offers examples that can be tailored depending on the needs of individual partnerships. It is important to have representation in the partnership from someone with expertise in the area of data analysis. Often, this can come from representatives from an institutional research department, or an academic unit within a partnering postsecondary institution, or from the assessment department at a school district. That partner could also potentially provide evaluation-type services, though external evaluation from an objective third party is always beneficial, since that entity would not have a stake in the success of the partnership.

This chapter provides information from several different efforts focused on creating indicator systems to understand student progress within and across systems. Each partnership will have different priorities, pain points, and areas of focus based on its desired goals and outcomes. For example, if the majority of students in a school do not pass a math placement test when they enter college, that high school would want to examine its math curriculum and look at how well it aligns with the content required in college-level courses and the placement examination at its partnering college. The partnering college would want to examine its placement processes to determine if they are measuring what is intended to be measured, in addition to stepping up its outreach to K–12 educators, students, and families. If affective, "noncognitive" surveys are administered and a high school learned that the majority of its students who matriculated into the partnering college are late getting to class and turning in assignments, the high school could focus its attention on supporting the development of time management and organizational skills in its student body. Thus, it is important to assess each partnership's work by using student-level data (data about each student). It is also important for data to be used to determine the area(s) of focus for the partnership to develop goals and objectives and decide on strategies, but this chapter focuses on how to assess effectiveness of the partnership work.

> Each partnership will have different priorities, pain points, and areas of focus based on its desired goals and outcomes.

Identifying indicators and collecting and sharing data are time and resource intensive. Involving experienced educational data analysts at the local level will greatly expedite the establishment of the data collection and reporting systems. Some partnerships use a "backbone" intermediary organization, such as a community or business organization with data expertise, to do this work. Data confidentiality agreements should be negotiated in accordance with the Family Educational Rights and Privacy Act (FERPA) and other state and local privacy protections. Although it is not true that FERPA prohibits the sharing of data among educational entities, educational institutions do need to protect student privacy and students' personally identifiable information. FERPA does allow for access to student data to increase accountability and transparency for educational outcomes and to contribute to a culture of continuous improvement in education (Data Quality Campaign, 2014). Do not let partnerships hit a roadblock with the privacy issues related to data sharing; there are valuable resources available to facilitate data sharing (see, e.g., the Data Quality Campaign website and the extensive resources related to FERPA at www.dataqualitycampaign.org/search/node/FERPA/).

Finally, much of the data analysis ends after high school; this is often the case because there are few longitudinal data systems in place to track students across education systems, and because, historically, college readiness efforts focused mostly on access to higher education. Many current partnerships are working to understand how well students progress through postsecondary education and transition into careers, and they are looking at a range of indicators to try to understand when students need interventions. The models that follow provide information about indicators to use in both high school and postsecondary environments.

Data Use Models

The crux of the data work is to select an indicator system that aligns to the desired goals and outcomes. This chapter highlights the work of three prominent models of college and career readiness indicators, including the work of the John W. Gardner Center at Stanford University; Cal-PASS Plus, a project of the Educational Results Partnership; and an augmentation of the Institute for Higher Education Leadership & Policy's (now EdInsights) indicators and milestones framework (the original was adopted for The California State University System's Student Success Dashboard). These are distinctly different frameworks that provide a broad range of examples that can be combined or adapted for individual contexts. The intent is that by providing examples of research-based data systems that are already in use, partnership teams will not need to reinvent the wheel and will be able to expedite the indicator selection process. The chapter ends with a discussion of a self-assessment tool made for high school/college partnerships.

> The intent is that by providing examples of research-based data systems that are already in use, partnership teams will not need to reinvent the wheel and will be able to expedite the indicator selection process.

College Readiness Indicator System (CRIS)

The John W. Gardner Center at Stanford University, with a grant from the Bill & Melinda Gates Foundation, developed the College Readiness Indicators Systems, or CRIS (http://gardnercenter .stanford.edu/resources/publications/Menu.CRIS.pdf). Based on extensive research examining the factors that predict students' readiness for college (note these indicators are for college readiness, and do not address explicitly address career readiness), CRIS focuses on three dimensions of readiness: Academic Readiness, Academic Tenacity, and College Knowledge at three different levels: individual students, schools, and systems. These three dimensions of readiness align to the Four Keys to College and Career Readiness: Academic Readiness includes key cognitive strategies

(Key 1: Think) and key content knowledge (Key 2: Know); Academic Tenacity addresses student ownership of learning aspects of the key learning skills and techniques (Key 3: Act); and College Knowledge incorporates key transitional knowledge and skills (Key 4: Go) and the learning techniques within the key learning skills and techniques (Key 3: Act). Within each of the three areas, the Gardner Center lists constructs or concepts to be measured, the indicators, and where such data could originate from—such as school records, teacher reports, or surveys. For the purposes of this book, Table 4.1 provides an abbreviated listing of indicators. For partnerships that wish to adopt the CRIS model, it is important to use the entire model and list of indicators and not pick and choose from the list.

The challenges with this system at the local level are how to construct surveys to administer and how to ensure that the administration does not contain biases or other problems that could skew the findings. There are climate surveys available online; for example, states often administer climate surveys annually. New Jersey's climate survey can be accessed here, for example, http://www.state.nj.us/education/students/safety/behavior/njscs/, along with template spreadsheets for analyses. There are also national school climate surveys focused on particular issues of interest, such as one developed by the Gay, Lesbian & Straight Education Network (http://glsen.org/nscs). Partnerships can pull items from different surveys, but be aware that sound surveys are carefully constructed to cover particular content, particular items (questions) are wordsmithed to ensure that all words will be understood the same way by different survey-takers, and care is taken to ensure that the questions are free of bias. Cutting and pasting from surveys is often not an effective approach, yet constructing a good survey from scratch is challenging, even for experienced survey developers.

Another challenge is that many of the interventions listed in the Gardner Center's online suite of tools can have more than one definition or set of components. For example, tutoring, mentoring, supplemental instruction, and other similar services can vary across different educational entities. Sources such as the U.S. Department of Education's What Works Clearinghouse (http://ies.ed.gov/ncee/wwc/) offer practice guides and other resources about *programs, products, practices,* and *policies* that meet certain levels of evidence—levels that meet the Department of Education's threshold for evidenced-based actions.

Table 4.1   CRIS Abbreviated Menu: Individual-, Setting- and System-Level Indicators

Indicators	Academic Readiness	Academic Tenacity	College Knowledge
Individual-Level Indicators	• GPA • No failures in core subjects • Completion of X-level math and science courses • Maintaining level of achievement in transition years • Performance on high school exit and benchmark exams • Participation in college-level coursework/college prep curriculum (AP, IB, Honors, etc.) • SAT/ACT scores	• Attendance • Disciplinary infractions • Mastery orientation[†] • Self-discipline[††]	• Knowledge of admission criteria, application process, and financial requirements for college • Completion and submission of applications to colleges that constitute a good match • Meeting with college adviser and/or having a postgraduation plan • Independent study skills (e.g., note taking and effective time management • SAT/ACT participation
Setting-Level Indicators	• Trends in individual-level indicators of academic preparedness • Teacher effectiveness/quality • Dropout rates (or high school completion rates)	• Trends in individual-level indicators of academic tenacity • Consistent attendance policy • Consistent disciplinary policy	• Trends in individual-level indicators of college readiness • High school college-going climate

(Continued)

Table 4.1 (Continued)

Indicators	Academic Readiness	Academic Tenacity	College Knowledge
	• Availability of college-level coursework/ college prep curriculum • Consistent grading policy	• Perceived safety of school • Instructional scaffolding[†††] • Academic press[††††] • Support for autonomy[†††††]	
System-Level Indicators	• Level of district/ state curricular requirements • Alignment of high school graduation requirements and college entry requirements • Resources allocated to efforts to promote college readiness • Monitoring system for schools' college attendance rates • Communication between district office and school personnel regarding college readiness	• Resources allocated to efforts to promote college readiness • Monitoring system for schools' college attendance rates • Communication between district office and school personnel regarding college readiness	• Policies that target the development of early college awareness and the skills to navigate the college and financial aid application process • Resources allocated to efforts to promote college readiness • Monitoring system for schools' college attendance rates • Communication between district office and school personnel regarding college readiness

Source: John W. Gardner Center (2014, p. 10).

[†]Mastery orientation, also known as learning orientation, refers to the desire to develop competence and improve one's skills.

[††]Self-discipline is the ability to forgo more appealing choices at the service of a higher goal.

[†††]Instructional scaffolding consists of providing students with assistance so that they can complete challenging tasks and activities.

[††††]Academic press refers to pushing students to work hard and to think hard.

[†††††]Autonomy is a sense of control over the course of one's life. Students are more successful when the adults in their lives support their need for autonomy rather than giving them little choice about how to think or behave.

Cal-PASS Plus: LaunchBoard

The CRIS model serves as a valuable starting point for selecting college readiness indicators. Partnerships also need to explore career readiness indicators. Cal-PASS Plus is a project in California that links student-level data regionally from pre-K through college and the workforce. It offers a wide range of analytical and facilitation-related services. The organization also organizes and facilitates regional learning councils that focus on issues such as the following:

- Improving academic achievement
- Determining the effectiveness of curriculum materials and instructional practices
- Closing the achievement gap
- Improving student transitions
- Increasing college readiness and success
- Facilitating the replication of best practices found in higher performing K–12 schools, community colleges, and four-year colleges and universities (www.calpassplus.org/CalPASS/ExploreDataAndCollaborate/RegionalLearningCouncils/About.aspx)

To help its partners and others across the state, Cal-PASS Plus houses several different kinds of data sets and tools. The project has developed a data reporting system with detailed employment-related indicators, so this section focuses on its CTE services. To assist its councils, Cal-PASS Plus recently developed its LaunchBoard to allow councils to learn about the scale, success, and labor market alignment of community college CTE program areas (www.calpassplus.org/Launchboard/LaunchboardDemo.aspx). The system allows for trends of up to five years to be examined. Program data include enrollments, capacity, support, student milestones, credentials, K–12 alignment, employment, and regional labor market information. For example, the employment indicators and methodology used to collect the data include the following:

- Employment: Students who complete a program and are employed in any field (self-employed, employed at one job, employed at two or more jobs; excludes respondents who indicated they transferred; includes program completers only)
- Employed in the same or similar field: job placement in the same or similar field of program of study

- Employment retention: count of students showing wages in at least one quarter in the first year after completion who also show wages in at least one quarter in the third year after completion
- Wage gain in the field: wage gain in a career that is the same or similar to the CTE educational pathway within the students' primary goal (self-employed, employed at one job, employed at two or more jobs; excludes respondents who indicated they transferred; includes program completers only)
- Average annual salary in the same or similar field: students who completed a program and are employed in a similar field as the program completed (self-employed, employed at one job, employed at two or more jobs; excludes respondents who indicated they transferred); wage gain above wages earned prior to completing the program
- Median annual salary for degree holders
- Median annual salary for certificate holders

Also, there is an additional tracking tool that can be used to understand students' participation in CTE activities that fall outside of traditional courses, such as K–12 career fairs.

Institute for Higher Education Leadership & Policy (IHELP; Now EdInsights)

The CRIS and the LaunchBoard system from Cal-PASS Plus provide strong examples of important indicators at the high school and postsecondary levels. This section provides an example of a pre-K through baccalaureate indicator system. In 2010, the Institute for Higher Education Leadership & Policy (IHELP) at California State University, Sacramento, now EdInsights, released a report commissioned by The Education Trust entitled *Advancing by Degrees* (Offenstein, Moore, & Shulock, 2010). In that report, IHELP proposed a research-based set of milestones and indicators that higher education administrators, staff, and faculty can track to help struggling students get the help they need. Milestones are measurable, intermediate, educational achievements that students reach on the path to completion. Indicators are academic patterns that predict the likelihood that students will reach the milestones. Those milestones and indicators are presented in Table 4.2.

IHELP posited that if colleges collected data about milestones and indicators and used that information to understand patterns of

Table 4.2   IHELP Milestones and Indicators

Milestones	Indicators

Retention:
 	
  Complete needed remediation
 	
  Transition to college-level coursework
 	
  Earn one year of college-level credits
 	
  Complete general education (GE)
 	
  Complete a community college transfer curriculum
 	
  Transfer from community college to university
  • Without completing curriculum
  • After completing curriculum
 	
  Complete certificate or degree
	Remediation:
	  Begin coursework in first year
	
	Gateway Courses:
	  Complete college-level math/ English in first year or two
	  Complete a college success course
	
	Credit Accumulation and Related Academic Behaviors:
	  Have a high rate of course completion
	  Complete 20–30 credits in first year
	  Earn summer credits
	  Enroll full time
	  Enroll continuously without stopping out
	  Register on time for courses
	  Maintain adequate academic performance

student behavior and achievement—and used that information to develop interventions to help students who face challenges associated with the milestones and indicators—institutions could help a larger proportion of students graduate. The California State University System adopted the milestones and indicators for its systemwide data dashboard. Venezia expanded the concept into pre-K–12 and, with the assistance of the doctoral students in her Winter 2014 Student Services course, created Table 4.3 to illustrate how the information could be used across education systems.

Table 4.3 likely needs to be tailored for each partnership, but it provides examples of the types of milestones and indicators that could be relevant for each grade/age.

Ultimately, the selection of indicators should be driven by the priorities of the partnership. Consider each goal, and then identify the desired outcomes to capture each goal. Then consider the key indicators, or interim leverage points, along the educational trajectory that impact the outcomes. The University of Chicago Consortium

Table 4.3 Pre-K Through 16 Milestones and Indicators

Education/ Grade Level	Milestone	Progress/ Success Indicator	Support Service(s)
Pre-K	Phonemic awareness Body control Appropriate social behavior Colors, shapes, words from a word bank	Read alphabet Sit while reading story Minimal conflict with peers, sharing	Preschool, reading support, Head Start, Transitional K, Mindfulness/ noncognitive exercises Family engagement
K–1	Sight words Reading comprehension Numbers 0–100 95% attendance Appropriate participation Appropriate/ constructive social/personal behavior/self-regulation	Words read to teacher/aide Story retold to teacher/aide Numbers read to teacher/aide Assessment Appropriate attendance Minimal conflict with peers and teachers, positive view of self	Reading and math specialists, individualized education plans (IEPs) Summer school Practical life skills Mindfulness/ noncognitive exercise Family engagement
2–3	More difficult sight words Reading comprehension Reading integration/ synthesis Inference Double digit numbers, addition, and subtraction Tests 95% attendance Appropriate/ constructive social/ personal behavior Science	Words read to teacher/aide Story retold to teacher/aide Response to questions requiring inference Numbers read and math completed for teacher/aide Appropriate scores on practice tests Assessment Minimal conflict with peers and teachers, positive view of self	Reading specialist, 504 plan, spelling bee, Response To Intervention (RTI) IEPs Math specialist, 504 plan, RTI Practice tests Mindfulness/ noncognitive exercises Science fair Art exhibition Mentoring/buddy Pen pals Tutoring

Education/ Grade Level	Milestone	Progress/ Success Indicator	Support Service(s)
	Art/performing arts 95% attendance 12 × 12 multiplication tables Appropriate use of technology Postsecondary/ career awareness Goal achievement	Learn about "college" and discuss different careers Goal determination	Afterschool program Field trips Tech supports in class Partner activities with postsecondary and workforce Culture of goal attainment Family engagement
4–6	Read for understanding Working well with peers Critical thinking abilities Multiplication tables Fractions Gateway classes Appropriate/ constructive social/personal behavior Science Art/performing arts/music 95% attendance Appropriate use of technology Postsecondary/ career awareness Goal achievement	Academic language Cooperative projects Practice, inference, synthesis, analysis Recitation of multiplication to teacher/aide Completion of fractions with teacher/aide Minimal conflict with peers and teachers, positive view of self Assessment Postsecondary visitation, career awareness, and job shadows Goal determination	Reading specialist, 504 plan, spelling bee, RTI IEPs Math specialist, 504 plan, RTI Mindfulness/ noncognitive exercises Science fair, art exhibition, music instruction Mentoring/buddy Pen pals Tutoring Afterschool program Field trips Computer lab/ supports Partner activities with postsecondary and workforce Culture of goal attainment Family engagement

(Continued)

Table 4.3 (Continued)

Education/ Grade Level	Milestone	Progress/ Success Indicator	Support Service(s)
7–9	Challenging courses Math completion leading to a challenging pathway in high school Effective essay writing "Promotion" from middle school Use of evidence effectively/ appropriately Brainstorm 10-year ed plan/life plan Critical thinking abilities Appropriate/ constructive social/personal behavior Science Art/performing arts/music 95% attendance Appropriate use of technology Postsecondary/ career awareness Goal achievement	Pre-Algebra in seventh grade, Algebra I in eighth grade, or Integrated Math I Writing/editing practice Sources cited appropriately Assessment- proficiency (such as SBAC in math and English Language Arts) Practice inference, synthesis, analysis, metacognition, critical evaluation, rhetorical skills Minimal conflict with peers and teachers, positive view of self Developing reflective practices Postsecondary visitation, summer school on postsecondary campus, job shadow, career exploration Goal determination	Advisor/teacher Math supports IEPs Writing supports Mindfulness/ noncognitive exercises Science fair, art exhibition, music instruction Tutoring Afterschool program Field trips Computer lab/ support Dietician Partner activities with postsecondary and workforce, financial aid info Culture of goal attainment Family engagement

Education/ Grade Level	Milestone	Progress/ Success Indicator	Support Service(s)
10–12	Tenth-grade (120 credits) Math completion in senior year Rigorous courses Critical thinking abilities Ten-year plans review (ed/life) Excellent writing abilities Excellent speaking/ listening skills Key assessments (PSAT SAT, etc.) 95% attendance FAFSA application Appropriate/ constructive social/personal behavior Science Art/performing arts/music Identification of likely college choices: "wish" institutes of higher education (IHEs), "like" IHEs, "backup" IHEs Appropriate use of technology Postsecondary/ career awareness Goal achievement	Successful midterm report cards Math enrollment for 12th grade Completion of rigorous coursework Practice inference, synthesis, analysis, metacognition, critical evaluation, rhetorical skills, persuasion Extended essay/ research paper Debate Assessment (includes practicing placement tests) Independent learning opportunities Work-based learning opportunities Community service Service learning projects Extracurriculars	Teacher as advisor/ advising, IEPs Math supports Capstone courses Senior projects Advancement Via Individual Determination- type programs Writing supports Speaking/listening coaching Test prep programs and services Career and technical education opportunities/ work-based learning Mindfulness/ noncognitive exercises Science fair, Project Lead The Way, art exhibition, music instruction Tutoring Afterschool program Field trips Computer lab/ support

(Continued)

Table 4.3 (Continued)

Education/ Grade Level	Milestone	Progress/ Success Indicator	Support Service(s)
		Minimal conflict with peers and teachers, positive view of self Dual enrollment, IHE visits to high school, internships Goal determination	Partner activities with postsecondary, financial aid information Culture of goal attainment Family engagement
13–14	Program of study selection Retention Needed remediation Transition to college-level coursework One year of college-level credits General education (GE) coursework Community college transfer curriculum Transfer from community college to a university • *After completing transfer curriculum* • *Without completing transfer curriculum* Certificate or degree completion	Remediation: • Remedial coursework in first term, if needed Gateway courses: • College-level math/ English within the first two years • College success course or other first-year experience program Credit accumulation and related academic behaviors: • *High ratio of course completion (low rate of course dropping and failure)*	Education plans First-year experience/ learning Advising Effective assessment, placement, and remediation practices Summer bridge Supplemental instruction Internship Student clubs Noncognitive supports Financial aid info Family engagement

Education/ Grade Level	Milestone	Progress/ Success Indicator	Support Service(s)
		• *Twenty to thirty credits in first year* • *Summer credits* • *Full-time enrollment* • *Continuous enrollment, without stop-outs* • *On-time registration for courses* • *Maintenance of adequate academic performance* Active engagement on campus	
Four-year postse condary institution	Credits from community college General Education courses completed Completion of 120 units Completion of each year Appropriate attendance and behavior Major chosen Career path chosen	Connected education plan and articulation agreement with community colleges Plan to complete General Education courses Education plan for remaining years and tracking of progress Instructor tracking of attendance and class behavior Appropriate course sequence Internships, apprenticeships, other work-based learning	Advising Writing center Math center Campus activities Noncognitive supports in tandem with instructor Online supports Summer school Connections with employers and graduate school opportunities, financial aid info Connections to community Family engagement

on Chicago School Research (2014) has identified the following four characteristics of effective indicators for college readiness:

1. Valid for the intended purpose

2. Actionable by schools

3. Meaningful and easily understood by practitioners

4. Aligned with the priorities of the district and schools

To address career readiness, an additional characteristic about addressing the desired career pathways and relevant partners external to the educational institutions should be considered. Partnerships could include information about students' career goals, along with data about, for example, badges and work-based learning accomplishments. By establishing an indicator system, all stakeholders will be able to monitor and make adjustments to the work over time. In addition, once the goals, outcomes, and indicators are determined, the programming that best supports the achievement of the goals, and the data to be collected, can be selected.

Self-Reflection and Assessment

Finally, one last aspect of data use relates to the effectiveness of the partnership. The partnership team itself should self-monitor the effectiveness of the efforts. The Career Ladders Project of the California Community Colleges, an organization that focuses on educational and career advancement, developed a tool to determine strengths and challenges to self-evaluate community college and K–12 partnerships (http://www.careerladdersproject.org/wp-content/uploads/2014/01/H2C-Partnership-Self-Assessment-Tool2.pdf). The tool has the following categories: systemwide data sharing, leadership engagement, cross-system staff collaboration, removal of access barriers, early college experiences and transition support, indicators of success of effective transition services, and college and career pathway development. Within each category are

> The partnership team itself should self-monitor the effectiveness of the efforts.

statements of promising practices that are then ranked as "never," "somewhat," "mostly," or "always/often." To illustrate this tool, the college and career pathways development section is listed in Table 4.4 to include additional information related to career readiness indicators.

Table 4.4   College and Career Pathway Development Self-Assessment

	Never	Somewhat	Mostly	Always/ Often
The high school career-focused pathways/programs and community college programs align to help students advance and accelerate in college and career options.				
Pathways are mapped to facilitate student understanding of seamless transitions and non-duplicative curriculum.				
Dual credit/dual enrollment opportunities are connected to or part of a pathway or sequence of study.				
Learning is aligned with industry-recognized certifications and stackable certificates, providing opportunity for students to build skills and a portfolio related to the career field.				
Pathways are developed in concert with regional employers from industry sector, and reflect in demand competencies and skills.				
Commonly developed pathway design provides integrated and rigorous CTE and academic content so that students reach milestones and earn certificates along the way to transfer.				
Students have the opportunity to earn and learn as they explore a career field; internships and other work-based learning opportunities are available to support the advancement in college and career.				

Source: Scolari and Antrobus (2014).

The next chapter describes how to select the programming to be included in this college and career readiness partnership work.

SUMMARY

Using data effectively can be a difficult challenge for partnerships. Analysis of student-level data drives not only the selection of areas on which to focus but also efforts to understand the effectiveness of the partnership. Some partnerships have a third party or intermediary organization conduct the analyses, since in-house expertise can be hard to find. The heart of this chapter focuses on presenting information from several models that can help partnerships frame their analytical work. The models are from the following organizations: the John W. Gardner Center at Stanford University; Cal-PASS Plus, a project of the Educational Results Partnership; and the Institute for Higher Education Leadership & Policy at California State University, Sacramento (now EdInsights).

DISCUSSION QUESTIONS

- Does your partnership have the capacity to connect individual, student-level data across education systems?
- Does your partnership include a person or organization that can house the data analytics for the effort and be viewed as impartial?
- Does your partnership analyze data to help pinpoint where students need help (to drive the work of the partnership)?
- Does your partnership build in the time necessary to reflect on its own processes, challenges, and strengths?

Taking Action

Too often, when working to improve education, we look for a silver bullet—a quick and easy way to solve a problem. Education is too complex an enterprise for a quick fix, and improving college and career readiness is no different. From organizational and logistical perspectives, college and career readiness efforts are incredibly complex because they require working across different educational systems. Ideally, such efforts also include involvement from across the community, including employers and community service providers. Simply adopting a promising practice, such as aligning assessments across educational systems, will not, in isolation, suffice to prepare all students to be college and career ready. Terry O'Banion (2011), a leading reformer from the community college arena, wrote that focusing on promising practices results in efforts that are "piecemeal, disconnected, and of short duration" (p. 29).

What is needed is a systemic framework to guide, connect, and embed the work across the secondary and postsecondary systems. A framework also helps all stakeholders get on the same page and makes the roles and responsibilities transparent. This chapter demonstrates how to use the Four Keys to College and Career Readiness (detailed in Chapter 2) as a framework to create a comprehensive plan for actions that need to be taken to achieve the goals (developed by the process described in Chapter 3) and the outcomes (identified by the process described in Chapter 4). In addition, this chapter categorizes the

> What is needed is a systemic framework to guide, connect, and embed the work across the secondary and postsecondary systems. A framework also helps all stakeholders get on the same page, and makes the roles and responsibilities transparent.

kinds of activities and approaches that a college and career readiness partnership can pursue. The chapter describes a two-step process to develop a comprehensive plan to improve college and career readiness: first, **identify and map existing efforts**; and second, analyze the map to create an **implementation plan** to guide the partnership's work.

Step 1: Map

One of the biggest challenges McGaughy noticed while conducting college and career readiness workshops around the country is not only the lack of coordination but also the lack of awareness of existing programs and activities in communities. A key theme running through this book is the reality that there are a lot of partnership efforts occurring across the country, but these efforts have great variance in scope, purpose, participation, and effectiveness. A lot of dedicated professionals are working very hard to improve educational outcomes for students. The challenge is to identify and leverage existing relationships and resources and build off of activities and programs already in place to create a seamless initiative. By using the Four Keys to College and Career Readiness as a conceptual lens to map current practice and guide future efforts, partnership teams can create a comprehensive plan addressing all areas needed for postsecondary readiness.

> The challenge is to identify and leverage existing relationships and resources and build off of activities and programs already in place to create a seamless initiative.

The problem of identifying and coordinating resources is particularly acute in large urban areas. For example, consider Los Angeles County: There are 80 public school districts, the Los Angeles Unified School District alone contains over 120 high schools, and the Los Angeles Community College District consists of nine colleges (LACCD, 2015), in addition to the multiple California State University campuses, the University of California at Los Angeles, and several dozen private two- and four-year colleges and universities. While conducting an introductory college and career readiness partnership workshop in Los Angeles sponsored by the California Community Colleges' Chancellor's Office, the participants began sharing and quickly realized there is so much going on throughout Los Angeles, and so many potential partners, that it is a struggle to determine how to develop an effective plan to improve college and career readiness. To begin the work, the participants organized themselves into regional teams (from "regions" within the greater Los Angeles metropolitan area) representing feeder patterns to the various community college campuses and then conducted the environmental scan described here.

To address the challenge of resource identification and coordination, McGaughy directed efforts at EPIC to assist partnerships in understanding existing efforts and identifying gaps. Termed an environmental scan, this approach helps stakeholders analyze current practices so a comprehensive plan can be implemented to improve college and career readiness. The goal of this process is to provide a starting point for contrasting "what is" with "what ought to be" (EPIC, 2007). Stakeholders are asked to investigate and identify at their home institutions current activities and programming. The information collected should include a description of the activity and who participates.

Stakeholders are then given a "map" to analyze activities in relation to the Four Keys to College and Career Readiness (see Table 5.1 for a hypothetical example of one local partnership involving 16 elementary schools, eight middle schools, four high schools, one community college, and one public university). The mapping tool was developed in 2011, when the Connecticut P–20 Council authorized EPIC to develop a *Connecticut College and Career Readiness Toolkit* (the toolkit with downloadable templates is available from www.ct.edu/files/pdfs/p20/p20-CT-Toolkit.pdf). This tool creates a map of current practices, helping to identify coverage, duplication, and gaps in formulating a comprehensive approach to improving college and career readiness.

After mapping the existing activities, the partners analyze the results. There are two key questions to be answered when reviewing the results of the environmental scan:

1. Are all Four Keys being addressed in the community?

2. Are all students having the opportunity to be prepared in all Four Keys ?

In the hypothetical example described in Table 5.1, the results indicate that programs and activities operating in the community do exist that address all Four Keys. However, there are some aspects of

Table 5.1   Sample Map of College and Career Readiness Activities

Think	Know
• *Project-based learning* (bie.org): teaching method incorporating extended learning opportunities implemented in 12 of 16 local elementary schools, 6 of 8 middle schools, and no high schools • *Research methods class:* required course for all ninth graders in school district plus required element of writing intensive freshman seminar at local university • *Senior Capstone Project:* required senior project and oral defense for seniors in three of four high schools • *Odyssey of the Mind* (www.odysseyof themind.com): international problem-solving competition used in four elementary schools (all students), two middle schools (all sixth graders and elective for seventh through eighth graders), one high school club team, and one community college team	• *Dual credit courses:* joint agreement between community college and all four high schools for students to earn college credits in high school with 50 percent student participation • *Career and technical education courses:* contextualized learning in real-world occupational areas with 100 percent of students taking one or more in one high school, with 75 percent at two others, and 50 percent at the fourth. • *Advanced placement* (AP; apcentral. collegeboard.com) or *International Baccalaureate* (IB; www.ibo.org): courses available in all high schools with 25 percent student participation • *Placement examinations:* one hundred percent of juniors in two high schools taking community college's placement exam; no students in other two high schools
Act	**Go**
• *Summer bridge program:* study and organizational skills and leadership development skills for 100 juniors for would-be first-generation college students offered by the state university • *WorkKeys* (www.act.org/products/ workforce-act-workkeys/): a job skills assessment for high school students to assess foundational and soft skills • *Advancement Via Individual Determination (AVID)* (www.avid. org): curriculum and instructional program (including note-taking, organization, and study skills) targeting increasing college readiness for students in the academic middle	• *Career planning:* all high school students required to develop and meet advisor annually to revise goals, course selection, workforce experiences, and plan • *College visits:* on-site college campus tours for seventh graders at one middle school; 50 percent of all high school sophomores visiting the community college; and all AP/IB students visiting the state university • *Financial aid clinic:* community college sponsoring financial aid clinic to assist with FAFSA preparation and scholarship searches available to all area high school students and families; approximately 50 families participating per year

available at two middle schools (25 students per grade), one high school (whole school model), and one community college course per semester • *Grit Intervention* (characterlab.org/research/current-projects): two middle schools participating in Character Lab intervention to teach students about deliberate practice	• *Internship program:* one high school partnering with local businesses to offer internships for juniors and seniors concentrating in either of two career cluster areas: health sciences or science; technology, engineering, and mathematics

the Four Keys that are not being addressed, such as motivation, collaborative learning, and technology within the Act key (see Chapter 2 for a complete description of the Four Keys). What is also missing is that not all students have the opportunity to access all of the existing programming. For example, although all students participate in career planning, only half of them participate in a college visit and only 50 families access the financial aid clinic. The stakeholders then list the gaps to identify what is needed for all students to be able to obtain the Four Keys.

Step 2: Plan

After completing the environmental scan, the partnership team will then have a road map of existing assets and gaps in programming. The next step is to develop a comprehensive action plan for implementing the necessary programming to achieve the desired goals. The *Connecticut College and Career Readiness Toolkit* also contains a downloadable template for a Comprehensive Partnership Plan (www.ct.edu/files/pdfs/p20/p20-CT-Toolkit.pdf). Elements that need to be addressed by the planning team include the following:

- Identification of the partnership activities organized by the Four Keys
- Goals and outcome measures addressed by each activity
- Resources available to support the activity
- Barriers to overcome and additional resources needed to support the activity
- Determination of next steps, including identifying responsible parties
- A timeline

This action plan then becomes the living document that not only guides the overall partnership work but the source for monitoring effectiveness, holding participants accountable, and making improvements and refinements to the work over time.

This action plan then becomes the living document that not only guides the overall partnership work but the source for monitoring effectiveness, holding participants accountable, and making improvements and refinements to the work over time.

The keys to this phase of work are the intentional selection of the activities and providers to be supported by the partnership. The eventual goal is to come up with a seamless array of services available to all students to prepare them for postsecondary success. The challenge is becoming aware of and sorting through all of the potential activities that could be undertaken. As noted previously, partnership-related programs and activities are ubiquitous around the country. Since 2007, McGaughy has collected a list of hundreds of college and career readiness activities encountered during her partnership workshops conducted around the country (see, e.g., the appendices in Conley et al., 2009; Conley, McGaughy, Ward, & Martinez, 2008). The authors analyzed this list and developed the following eight categories of strategies, activities, and programs to aid partnership teams in selecting desired interventions for implementation. The hope is to streamline the sharing of ideas and strategies and realize that most likely others have developed similar programming to what is desired. In other words, partnership efforts do not need to "reinvent the wheel" but can learn and adapt from the work of others. The following section describes the eight categories and provides illustrative examples.

Category 1: Building a College and Career Readiness Culture

To equip students for postsecondary readiness, the entire community (including families, educators, employers, and community members) must support and value college and career readiness through both symbolic and substantive ways. Educational institutions, with direct community involvement, should "habitually engage in behaviors and practices that demonstrate the pervasive schoolwide belief that all students can enroll in postsecondary education after high school graduation and be successful" (Conley, 2010, p. 105). The adults in the community hold high expectations for all students, valuing and celebrating both career and college-focused options. The messaging needs to counter the historical belief that "not all students will go to college" with "all of our students will be prepared for success after high school." There are many creative ideas happening around the country to foster a college and career readiness culture. Some examples of culture building activities include the following:

- Development of a shared vision and goal setting (see Chapter 3)
- Mobilization for community engagement, including grassroots organizing and information sharing
- Communication tools for advocacy and messaging (e.g., college access marketing at www.collegeaccessmarketing.org)
- Rituals: career fairs and college signing days
- Symbols: career profiles of successful alumni hung in hallways, alumni plaques with college attended and degrees earned, and college banners.

The leadership team for the partnership should engage marketing and communications experts in the community to spearhead this work and tailor the messaging to local interests and priorities.

Generation Texas

In October 2010, the Texas Higher Education Board launched regional Generation Texas efforts in Fort Worth and San Antonio and has expanded the work to include 10 regions in Texas. These regional efforts target students, parents, educators, and businesses and community leaders to join the "movement" to accomplish three key goals:

- To develop a commitment among stakeholders to create a college-going culture in Texas public schools that prepares all students for a postsecondary education.
- To clarify the processes of applying for admission and student financial aid.
- To increase awareness of and build support for the Texas College and Career Readiness Standards.

The Generation Texas website (http://gentx.org) offers an array of powerful stories, resources, events, and marketing materials for communities to use to inspire and inform students to be college and career ready.

Source: Texas Higher Education Coordinating Board (2012).

Category 2: Developing Lifelong Adaptable Learners

Student academic preparation and curriculum and instruction must be aligned to a college and career readiness trajectory to ensure that students graduate with the knowledge and skills they need to successfully engage in postsecondary learning environments. The root of the preparations gap stems from a disjointed educational system. Educators have historically worked in silos, creating great variance in expectations and requirements for student learning. How can students be prepared for postsecondary learning when the educational system has not explicitly determined nor systematically taught what students need to know and be able to do? This category of work is critically important but complex. Chapter 6, "Aligning Curricula Across Educational Systems," discusses how local partnerships can collaborate to align what students should know and be able to do. Here are examples of strategies and activitiesto improve students' successful academic preparation for collegeand careers:

- Curriculum alignment throughout K–12 to college and career readiness standards (e.g., www.engageny.org/common-core-curriculum)
- Multidisciplinary integrated curriculum that connects theoretical knowledge and real-world applications (e.g., linked learning at connectedcalifornia.org)
- Inclusion of subjects outside the academic core (such as CTE, art, music, and so forth)
- Inclusion of the key cognitive strategies and key learning strategies and techniques (e.g., noncognitive factors such as attribution, persistence, resiliency, grit, etc.; see Conley, 2013)
- Professional development for preservice and in-service teachers
- Scoring calibration/moderation activities between secondary and postsecondary faculty, including shared rubrics and exemplars
- Test preparation for college entrance and placement examinations (e.g., have all high school juniors take local community college placement examinations and use the senior year to remediate those in need)
- Development of paired courses for exit-level high school and entry-level college courses (see sidebar of South Carolina Course Alignment Project)

This category of activities and programs addresses the academic preparation of students for college and career readiness. A critical element that cannot be overlooked is that this area includes more than key content knowledge (Key 2: Know) but also the key cognitive strategies (Key 1: Think) and key learning skills and techniques (Key 3: Act). A consequence of the era of high-stakes testing has been a narrowing of the curriculum to a focus on basic knowledge and skills that are assessed on standardized tests. To achieve college and career readiness, students require more than just the basics. To develop flexible and adaptable lifelong learners, students need academic preparation aligned to a college and career readiness trajectory that integrates thinking and learning skills with rich content and opportunities for creativity and applied and contextual learning.

South Carolina Course Alignment Project (SCCAP)

In an effort to improve alignment between high school courses and entry-level college courses, teachers and administrators across South Carolina work together to ensure seamless transitions for students. Beginning in 2008, the South Carolina Commission on Higher Education has partnered with EPIC to create a regional network of high school and college faculty creating "paired courses." A paired course is an exit-level high school course that is deliberately designed to align with an entry-level college course in the same curricular area. These sequenced courses promote a seamless transition for students from high school to postsecondary education. The goals of the project are to

- improve high school graduation rates, reduce the need for remedial instruction in college, and improve college retention and graduation rates;
- use a statewide framework that supports local solutions;
- strengthen faculty resources by creating regional networks of professional educators who can share ideas, collaborate, and modify their current policies and practices as they learn how to prepare all students for postsecondary success; and
- create clear pathways between high school and college coursework to reduce curriculum redundancy between high school and college.

To date, 11 paired courses in English Language Arts, mathematics, and science have been created (for more information, please see www .epiconline.org/south-carolina-alignment-project). The paired courses are

(Continued)

(Continued)

intentionally designed as a sequential curriculum between the senior year of high school and the freshman year of college. Participating faculty members work collaboratively in their geographic regions to meet regularly, use each other as content resources in their regional groups, teach paired courses together, and conduct classroom visits.

Source: Educational Policy Improvement Center (2013).

Category 3: Exploring Aspirations

Students cannot aspire to or plan effectively for futures about which they lack sufficient knowledge. Broadening horizons, tied to the opportunities available in the community, enables students to truly achieve their aspirations. This is not meant to advocate a replication of a tracking system that forces students to choose a career at a young age. In the words of Conley (2013), "The goal is not to have students pick occupations, but to have them begin to make stronger connections between what they are learning and what they are interested in doing with their lives" (p. 44). Career exploration and work-based learning opportunities enable students to see how what they are learning in the classroom is connected to the real world and to explore career options to help motivate and improve their ownership of learning. Examples of career exploration activities include the following:

- CTE pathways (e.g., Achieve Texas at www.achievetexas.org)
- Career interest surveys (e.g., O*NET Interest Profiler at www .mynextmove.org)
- A range of work-based learning opportunities (e.g., linked learning at linkedlearning.org/linked-learning-in-action/work-based-learning/)
- Professional mentors
- Career presentations
- Internships
- Job shadowing
- Enrichment programs (e.g., C-STEM Teacher and Student Support Services, www.cstem.org)

Increasing students' awareness of career options also has an important equity component. Students who come from communities that have historically not had representative access to certain career areas may never have heard about certain opportunities or may not have met anyone in particular career fields. Expanding the students' awareness and their ability to personally interact with professionals from various professions enables students to envision a broader range of possibilities for their future.

Boston Private Industry Council (PIC) Career Exploration

The Boston Private Industry Council (PIC) is a nonprofit organization that connects business, the Boston Public Schools, higher education, government, labor, and community organizations to create innovative workforce and education solutions that benefit Boston residents and businesses alike. As an intermediary or the "glue" in partnerships, the PIC (a) convenes local leadership around education and workforce priorities, (b) brokers employer partnerships, (c) connects youth and adults with education and employment opportunities, and (d) measures program impact, in terms of both quality and scale. The Boston PIC organizes a range of career exploration programs to help high school students understand the career opportunities available to them after completing school. Employers participate in these programs, whether at the workplace or the school, so that the experience is real for the students. Students and employers, alike, often take part in one of these initiatives before participating in a summer job or internship. Career exploration programs supported by the PIC include the following:

- **Job Shadow Day:** This is a half-day event designed to expose high school students to the world of work. Students "shadow" professionals during a normal workday to gain a firsthand look at the skills, knowledge, and education required to succeed in a career.
- **Mock Interviews:** Students have the opportunity to practice interviewing and sharpen their skills, which is critical due to the competitive labor market for teenagers.
- **Career Speakers:** Professionals from a wide variety of occupations share their career story with high school students, during one class or over the course of a semester.

For more information and related resources, see www.bostonpic.org/programs/career-exploration.

Source: Boston Private Industry Council.

Category 4: Navigating the Future

To prepare effectively for their future, students need access to what has historically been privileged knowledge to successfully develop actionable college and career goals. This privileged knowledge (such as familiarity with the differences among postsecondary institutions regarding admissions requirements, application procedures, etc.) is a significant barrier for students who are potential first-generation college attenders or come from communities that historically have not had representative access to postsecondary education. The role of the partnership is to provide this information in a timely manner to all students, regardless of background. This includes providing procedural information, such as knowing what courses to take as part of a program of study to pursue a desired career path, exploring postsecondary options, and knowing requirements and deadlines for admissions. Activities to help students successfully navigate their future include the following:

- Career path development (e.g., Programs of Study: Local Implementation Readiness and Capacity for Self-Assessment, a Tool for Local College and Career Readiness by MPR Associates [2010], cte.ed.gov/docs/POSLocalImplementationTool-9-14-10.pdf)
- College options and matching (e.g., College Search Step-By-Step from the College Board at bigfuture.collegeboard.org/find-colleges/how-to-find-your-college-fit/college-search-step-by-step)
- General school counseling
- An advisory curriculum
- College visits
- A briefing on admissions procedures
- Placement preparation
- Registration assistance
- Academic advising
- Course selection (both secondary and postsecondary)
- Transition services (e.g., summer bridge programs or academies)
- Orientation
- Peer mentoring

Beyond procedural information, another important element to prepare students for postsecondary readiness is the culture of many college campuses. Again, potential first-generation college attenders or students from communities historically with limited access to college or certain career areas may not have experience navigating the culture on a college campus or in an unfamiliar work environment.

The differences can be intimidating and alienating, and our institutions often view students through the lens of a deficit model (what students do not know) as opposed to an attribute model (what students can bring to the table). Many of these vulnerable students experience "impostor syndrome"—the belief that they may not really belong in the new environments and will be exposed as frauds (Wier, 2013). Instead of self-advocating for needed assistance (such as organizing a study group or going to an academic help center), students often further isolate themselves for fear of exposure. An important aspect of preparing all students, particularly the most vulnerable, is to support the development of their cultural and social capital—in particular, the ability to successfully navigate the prevailing norms and interpersonal relationships (Goldring, Cohen-Vogel, & Smrekar, 2003). This includes making sure all students gain exposure, interactions, familiarity, and relationships with role models, peers, and representatives from the desired postsecondary setting and empowering them to self-advocate and seek assistance as needed. It is also critically important for postsecondary institutions to rethink the deficit model framework and implement new ways to provide services, such as implementing one-stop student support centers (to lessen the feelings of stigmatization for students seeking services); integrating academics and student supports; and providing light touch interventions and other forms of support to all or most students.

College App Map

In 2012, College Summit and the King Center Charter School joined the Bill & Melinda Gates Foundation to launch the College Knowledge Challenge, a $2.5 million fund to develop innovative apps on Facebook that will help students apply to, attend, and stay in college. The goal of the challenge is to make the college-going process more transparent, collaborative, and easy to navigate for low-income and first-generation students. The result of this competition is the College App Map (collegeappmap .org), where students can find apps to support, inform, and coach them to and through college. The map shows the tasks or "steps" students have to achieve each year in high school and college to stay on the path to success. Next to each step, students will find the name of an app that helps them achieve that step. The apps help students explore careers, choose a college, identify how to pay for college, review strategies for how to succeed in college, and they also offer some all-in-one tools.

Source: College Summit (2014).

Federal Student Aid (an office of the U.S. Department of Education)

The Internet is rife with information about financial aid for college—entering the search term "college financial aid" using Google returns over 61 million results. A valuable starting point is the U.S. Department of Education's Office of Federal Student Aid's comprehensive website (see studentaid.ed.gov). This website provides a strong foundational understanding of financial literacy, the process and options for obtaining aid, and a list of resources. Information is organized by categories to explain how students should prepare for college, what types of aid are available, how to qualify and apply for aid, and how to manage student loans. The website includes checklists, fact sheets, videos, numerous links for federal, state, and college information, and announcements for current financial aid opportunities.

Category 5: Financing the Future

Different career pathways and postsecondary settings have different costs. Helping students and parents/guardians navigate financial decisions is critical for students to make informed choices to achieve their aspirations. In particular, potential first-generation college attenders and low-income families need access to financial information and counseling to ensure the postsecondary training and education are within reach. For example, awareness of and the complexity of filling out the Free Application for Federal Student Aid (FAFSA) can be a barrier for some families. Some of the important financial information necessary for all students to access includes the following:

- Individualized assistance with financial aid, including help for parents/guardians
- Financial literacy
- Career salaries (e.g., the Salary Surfer, created by the California Community College Chancellor's Office, salarysurfer.cccco.edu/SalarySurfer.aspx)
- Costs of different postsecondary options (e.g., online comparisons of college costs and reported salaries upon graduation such as NerdWallet, www.nerdwallet.com/nerdscholar/compare-colleges-and-pay)
- FAFSA workshops and information (e.g., the National Association for Student Financial Aid Administrators' "FAFSA Tips and Common Mistakes to Avoid," www.nasfaa.org/students/About_Financial_Aid.aspx)
- Scholarships (full, partial, close-the-gaps, technology)
- Debt management

Unraveling the actual costs associated with attending college is a complex process. The process includes knowing how to select the appropriate postsecondary learning opportunity (such as the military, apprenticeships, college, etc.); knowing when and how to fill out the FAFSA if financial aid is necessary; applying for other grants, scholarships, and loans; and considering work-study jobs, internships, and part-time employment. All families, but particularly low-income families, need assistance in making these difficult decisions with potential long-term financial consequences. Local high school and college partnerships can serve as a clearinghouse for coordinating the local expertise in promoting financial literacy for all students.

Category 6: Accelerating Learning Opportunities for All Students

Blurring the boundaries between high school and beyond enables more students to obtain career aspirations more efficiently. High schools and postsecondary institutions around the country are offering a wide variety of opportunities for students to earn certificates and college credit in high school. There are multiple benefits to such arrangements, such as saving time and money by earning credentials or credits while still in high school and obtaining a deeper understanding of postsecondary expectations. There are a variety of approaches to providing accelerated learning opportunities, including the following:

- Dual/concurrent enrollment or dual credit courses (academic and CTE; this book uses the term "dual enrollment")
- Industry certificates and credentials earned in high school
- AP or IB courses
- Online courses
- Early and middle college high schools (e.g., Middle College National Consortium, mcnc.us)

Commonly used around the country, dual enrollment programs allow high school students to simultaneously earn credit toward a high school diploma and a postsecondary degree or certificate. Dual enrollment programs vary in terms of how they are financed, who can participate, where the courses are offered, who teaches the courses, types of enrolled students, and how many courses are offered through the program. For example, courses can be offered on a college campus or at a high school. Courses can be taught by college faculty or by high school teachers certified by the college. Some dual enrollment programs teach high school students separately, while others combine high school students and college students in the same course. With such variation, challenges for partnerships are to oversee and monitor the consistency and quality of the course offerings.

Early College Designs

Developed by Jobs For the Future (JFF), Early College Designs (www.early-colleges.org) blend high school and college, compressing the time it takes to complete a high school diploma and the first two years of college. Early college students are outperforming their peers nationwide:

- Ninety percent graduate high school compared with 78 percent of students nationally.
- Ninety-four percent earn free college credit while in high school.
- Thirty percent earn an associate's degree or other postsecondary credential while in high school.

Since 2002, JFF and partners around the country have helped start or redesign nearly 250 Early College Schools that currently serve more than 75,000 students nationwide. Early College High Schools replace remediation with accelerated curricula and individualized supports to prepare all students—particularly those traditionally underserved—for college and careers. The Early College network includes a range of Early College designs, including the following:

- Full-service Early College High Schools
- Early College STEM (science, technology, engineering, and mathematics) schools
- Early College pathways in comprehensive high schools
- "Pathways to Prosperity" models that integrate career pathways with an associate's degree
- "Back on Track" models that reengage off-track and out-of-school youth

Early College Designs are based on the idea that academic rigor, combined with the opportunity to save time and money toward a postsecondary credential, are powerful motivators for students, while additional supports help students' efforts in meeting expectations.

Source: Jobs for the Future (2014).

Category 7: Providing Integrated Student Support Services

All students have unique needs. To support student success, a holistic approach to assisting students in meeting their individual circumstances is necessary. Support services are intended to increase students' chances to succeed in all levels of education (Weissman et al., 2009). In higher education, there are departments or divisions dedicated to providing services and support to enhance student growth and development (physical, mental, and emotional), often called Student Affairs. Postsecondary institutions typically offer a wide range of supports but with varying usage. As optional services, many students, particularly first-generation students who tend to need the services the most, do not access them (Karp, O'Gara, & Hughes, 2008). Often, there is a stigma attached to seeking services. Analyzing the student support needed as part of a comprehensive action plan for college and career readiness, then, needs to consider both the availability of needed services and outreach to ensure the students most in need of services are accessing them. Some examples of support services include the following:

- Case management
- Personal counseling and socioemotional support services
- Writing/math/computer or other academic centers
- Tutoring
- Adult education
- Dropout transition services
- Wraparound services
- Referrals to community agencies
- Coordinated outreach/collaboration with community partners
- Transportation
- Child care
- Life skills

There is a movement, particularly among community colleges, to ensure that support services become a more integrated part of students' ongoing experiences in courses and in other aspects of college life, rather than an option that students have to actively seek out independently (Dadgar, Nodine, Bracco, & Venezia, 2013). In the federal government, through the Student Support Services (SSS) grants, the U.S. Department of Education (U.S. DoED) is requiring the integration of academics with SSS for grant recipients (U.S. DoED, 2015). This integration movement should be addressed by the college and career readiness partnership efforts. The eight categories of partnership activities described in this chapter should not be considered as work to be done in silos. Student support efforts should be fully integrated with the other strategies and activities undertaken to create college and career ready students.

Accelerated Study in Associate Programs (ASAP) at the City University of New York (CUNY)

Launched in 2007 with support from the New York City Center for Economic Opportunity, ASAP began as a comprehensive program designed to increase significantly increase the graduation rates of associate-degree students at six CUNY community colleges. Key program components include full-time enrollment in select majors, block scheduled first-year courses, cohort course taking, financial support, intrusive and mandatory advisement, a student success seminar, career services, and tutoring. The program is committed to graduating at least 50 percent of students within three years through the provision of comprehensive support services and financial resources (i.e., textbook assistance, NYC MetroCards, and tuition waivers to cover any balance between financial aid and tuition/fees) that remove barriers to full-time study, build student resiliency, and support timely degree completion.

To date, there have been seven cohorts served to date involving 6,400 students, with more than double the graduation rates of similar students: After three years, 47 percent of ASAP students with developmental needs and 56 percent of fully skilled proficient ASAP students have graduated versus 19 percent and 28 percent of non-ASAP students, respectively. The program just admitted an eighth cohort of 4,300 students in fall 2014 and, thanks to support from the New York City Office of the Mayor, will expand to serve 13,000 students by academic year 2016–2017. This program has been rigorously evaluated using multiple methods, including a random experimental design and a cost benefit analysis (for a description of the studies, see www1.cuny.edu/sites/asap/evaluation/).

Some of the findings include the following:

- There are large and significant differences between ASAP and comparison group students in terms of retention rates, movement through developmental education, credit accumulation, and graduation rates.

- Students from underrepresented groups appear to benefit more from ASAP than other students.
- Although up-front costs are higher, the average cost per three-year ASAP graduate is, on average, $6,500 lower than comparison group graduates; for every dollar invested in ASAP by the taxpayer, $3.50 is returned per associate degree in increased tax revenues and social service savings; and for each dollar invested by the ASAP students, $12.20 is returned through increased earnings.

For more detail, see www.cuny.edu/asap.

Source: City University of New York (2014).

Category 8: Organizing, Governing, and Measuring Success

Partnership efforts must have a structure and the capacity to support the work. Partnering is a process, not a program. As described in Chapter 3, "Organizing the Partnership," this process starts by establishing a leadership team with decision-making and resource allocation authority. This leadership team also identifies the work groups and individuals that will then carry out the work of the partnership. The process for sustaining the work also includes a focus on collecting and sharing data and monitoring the effectiveness of the work (discussed in Chapter 4). Some operational elements that must be addressed to organize and maintain the partnership include the following:

- Leadership capacity (see also Chapter 7 describing decision makers, implementers, and champions)
- Staffing capacity
- Joint strategic planning
- Resources (e.g., time, materials, and place)
- A needs assessment (such as the action planning process described in this chapter)
- Monitoring and evaluation
- Data sharing for improvement (e.g., Cal-PASS Plus, an accessible, actionable, and collaborative pre-K through 16 system of student data available at www.calpassplus.org)
- Cross-system communication (see also Chapter 7 describing the development of a communication strategy)

There are different models for organizing partnerships' work. One approach uses an intermediary organization to facilitate or support the partnership process (see, e.g., the following sidebar about StriveTogether). Another approach has one of the institutions taking the lead in facilitating the work, such as at the local community college. For example, in Illinois, a frequently mentioned successful college and career readiness partnership approach is referred to as the "Elgin Model." Since 2006, Elgin Community College has partnered with feeder school districts to form the Alliance for College Readiness. An advisory council oversees the efforts of seven work teams: reading; writing; math; STEM; English Language Learners (ELL); Supporting Transition, Engaging Parents (STEP); and a kindergarten team (Schaid, 2014, p. 2). Another example, Alignment Nashville, is distinct because of its wide range of committees—over 20—focused on issues such as behavior, caring adults, unemployed youth, health, pre-K, experiential learning, and parent engagement (www.alignmentnashville.org). All committees have agreed on processes and principles, demonstrating how a complex network of partners can be organized.

These approaches have advantages and disadvantages. A main advantage of using an intermediary is that it can be viewed as neutral and not favoring any one particular institution. A disadvantage is it can be viewed as an outsider, with no lasting authority. A major advantage of having one of the institutions facilitate the partnership is that the work is part of and has direct access to the system. A disadvantage is that it can be viewed as biased toward favoring the sponsoring institution over the other partners. The ultimate decision needs to come from the leadership team. Which model works the best in terms of the local context, that is, the history, the resources, and the preexisting relationships and trust?

StriveTogether Approach

StriveTogether, a subsidiary of KnowledgeWorks, is a national network of more than 50 community partnerships using a collective impact approach to create local educational ecosystems to support children and youth from cradle to career. StriveTogether's Theory of Action offers a rigorous collective impact approach to help communities develop the cradle to career civic infrastructure needed to change systems and have sustainable impact on student outcomes. The Theory of Action is built on four principles:

1. **Engage the community:** Work with a broad array of community voices to create unified educational strategies and solutions.

2. **Focus on eliminating locally defined disparities:** Use local data to identify inequalities in student achievement and prioritize efforts to improve student outcomes.

3. **Develop a culture of continuous improvement:** Use local data, community expertise, and national research to identify areas for constant, disciplined improvement.

4. **Leverage existing assets:** Build on and align existing community resources to maximize the impact of the work.

The core focus of this approach is using data to determine what works best for children. StriveTogether experts support communities in developing shared outcomes and indicators of success to use across programs and systems, identifying promising practices, and allowing for meaningful dialogue about local disparities and solutions to close achievement gaps. They provide tools such as the Civic Infrastructure Assessment to help communities determine the unique strengths and obstacles and the Theory of Action Gateways and the annual Progress Assessment that offer a specific progression of quality benchmarks that are necessary for sustained impact and improvement over time. For more detail, see www.strivetogether.org.

Source: Knowledge Works Foundation (2014).

As demonstrated by the examples included in each of the eight categories of partnership activities, there are many different options that pathways can use. The purpose of this book is to provide partnerships with the frameworks, processes, and strategies to make intentional choices to create a comprehensive array of supports aligned to the Four Keys to College and Career Readiness. The action plan should address all Four Keys, reduce duplication of efforts, and address gaps in content coverage and missing students. The action planning process should include the phases of work. Undertake the "low hanging fruit" first, meaning start with programming already in existence or what would be the easiest to implement communitywide. For example, in the hypothetical community described in the environmental scan in Table 5.1, the initial phase of work might include replicating the financial aid clinics on each high school campus and expanding college campus visits and internship opportunities for juniors and seniors from all high schools in the school districts. Over time, additional phases should be planned to further expand programs and activities so that all Four Keys are being addressed for all students.

SUMMARY

Simply adopting a promising practice, such as aligning assessments across educational systems, will not suffice to prepare all students to be college and career ready. In addition, many communities are unaware of the myriad of programming already in existence to support students. This chapter demonstrates how to use the Four Keys to College and Career Readiness as a framework to create a comprehensive partnership plan. The chapter describes a two-step process to develop a comprehensive plan to improve college and career readiness. First, partnerships can identify and map existing efforts; second, they can analyze the map to create a comprehensive implementation plan. The eventual goal is to come up with a seamless array of services available to all students to prepare them for postsecondary success. The challenge is becoming aware of and sorting through all of the potential activities that could be undertaken. This chapter details eight categories of strategies, activities, and programs to aid partnership teams in selecting desired interventions for implementation. Partnership efforts do not need to "reinvent the wheel" but can learn and adapt from the work of others. The action plan should address the provision of all Four Keys for all students, reduce the duplication of efforts, and close the gaps in access.

DISCUSSION QUESTIONS

- Are all of the partners aware of all of the major activities and programs available within and across educational systems? With workforce partners?
- Does your partnership weigh or value all aspects of the Four Keys similarly? Are any more important than the others?
- Are there existing strategies, activities, or programs available that address all Four Keys? What is missing?
- Do all students have access to strategies, activities, or programs that address all Four Keys? If not, which students do not have access to which keys?
- Do some students, or groups of students, have unique needs that should be addressed to help them overcome barriers for postsecondary readiness? What additional supports from the eight categories of activities are needed to meet these needs?

Aligning Curricula Across Educational Systems

A root of the preparation gap high school graduates face stems from a disjointed educational system (Venezia et al., 2003). As described in Chapter 1, historically the K–12 and postsecondary educational systems operated in silos. These different sectors have established their own expectations and requirements for learning objectives, assessment, graduation, and admissions, creating great variance both within and between educational systems. Students often face an eclectic muddle of coursework during their high school years and first years of college (Grades 10–14), until they select a college major (Kirst & Usdan, 2009). To address this gap between high school and college preparation, this chapter describes how local partnerships can collaborate to align what students are expected to know and be able to do. This process involves teams of educators working together to examine and refine what is being taught and to build seamless learning pathways for each successive year of education, culminating with students arriving at their desired postsecondary setting prepared to succeed in entry-level coursework.

> These different sectors have established their own expectations and requirements for learning objectives, assessment, graduation, and admissions, creating great variance both within and between educational systems.

The purpose of this chapter is two-fold: first, to provide an overview of the alignment field so local educators obtain a deeper understanding of this complex area, and second, to provide a "how-to" guide for local teams of high school and college instructors to partner to align curriculum, focused on college and career readiness. This chapter is based on a toolkit, developed by McGaughy's team (McGaughy, van der Valk, Singleton, Zalewski, & Farkas, 2012) at EPIC, for the Illinois Community College Board, the Illinois Board of Higher Education, and the Illinois State Board of Education. The toolkit, titled "Bridging the Gap: An Illinois Toolkit for Using the Common Core for Secondary and Postsecondary Alignment," was created for educators at both the secondary and postsecondary levels to both increase familiarity with the Common Core and be used as a foundation to create curricula aligned to college and career readiness expectations. The ultimate goal, for both this chapter and for the original toolkit, is through meaningful local partnerships that students will progress successfully along a college and career readiness trajectory and arrive prepared for postsecondary programs.

Getting Started

The first step in the toolkit is to focus on closing the academic preparation gap for postsecondary readiness by forming vertical teams of subject area faculty members. Vertical teams consist of faculty members representing both high school and college departments, ideally chaired by department heads or curriculum specialists. This work typically begins with mathematics and English Language Arts (ELA) to reduce remedial or developmental education placements for entry-level students. The vertical teaming can then branch into other subjects, including CTE areas, depending on local priorities and needs.

During the kick-off meeting for the vertical teams, members first must all be on the same page about the need and rationale for the work. A powerful way to jump-start and frame the work is through data sharing. Postsecondary representatives can bring data reports about placement testing results sorted by high school. In addition, vertical team members can each take a sample placement examination used by the participating postsecondary institutions so they obtain firsthand knowledge of what entering students encounter. In mathematics, many instructors realize that students are taught the required content assessed in the placement examinations, but the content might have been taught in middle schools (such as multiplying and dividing fractions). Equally important is for postsecondary faculty to examine what is being required in high school. Postsecondary representatives also need to become familiar with high school exit standards and consider what the high schools are being held accountable for teaching. For ELA and math, the high school exit standards currently used in 43 states are the high school level of the Common Core. In the other seven states, please refer to the required exit-level high school standards (such as the Texas College and Career Readiness Standards). Throughout this chapter, the term "targeted standards" is used to refer to these high school exit-level standards, representing the culminating knowledge and skills high school graduates need to be college and career ready. The overall guiding question for the vertical team members is this: "Does what we currently teach match (align) with what is required both at the high school and college levels?"

Types of Alignment

Another important initial step for the vertical teams is obtaining a clear understanding of alignment. The concept of alignment is the coordination and calibration of educational components to the required knowledge and skills. The required knowledge and skills for K–12 educators are prescribed in the state standards. The required knowledge and skills for postsecondary faculty are usually their institutional and departmental student learning objectives. These requirements represent the minimum requirements; instructors at both levels can teach additional knowledge and skills as desired.

Occurring concurrently, there are two ways vertical teams must approach alignment work. *Vertical alignment* refers to curriculum that builds sequentially on the content and performance expectations taught in each course, from year to year, moving students along a trajectory that culminates at the college and career readiness level. *Horizontal alignment* refers to consistency across similar course titles and levels for students, resulting in a student having the opportunity to learn similar content and expectations regardless of which instructor is teaching the course. As the vertical teams conduct their alignment work, the instructors must be working collaboratively across grade levels/course sequences and within their own grade/course levels to ensure both vertical and horizontal alignment.

Overall, tackling the misalignment between high school and college requires a deep examination about the way the requirements (standards and learning objectives) are addressed at each level. This examination is conducted using standards alignment analyses. This refers to the relationship, or the degree of match, between the desired standards and the related educational component being examined, including four types of standards alignment analyses:

1. *Standard to standard alignment* refers to an analysis between two or more sets of standards. There are many different methods, with varying levels of sophistication, to conduct standard to standards alignment studies. At the national level, EPIC conducted an alignment study examining the relationship between the exit-level Common Core and each of five sets of existing standards (California and Massachusetts state standards, the Texas College and Career Readiness Standards, the Knowledge and Skills of University Success, and the International Baccalaureate Diploma Programme). The report found a substantial content match and consistency between the cognitive challenge level with the Common Core and the comparison standards (Conley et al., 2011b). In addition, most states, upon adopting the Common Core, created crosswalks to determine which of the old standards matched with the Common Core in regard to skills and concepts, performance expectations, and grade-level timing (for example, in the state of Oregon, for ELA, see www.ode.state.or.us/search/page/?id=3356, and for math, see www.ode.state.or.us/search/page/?=3211). In short, depending on the location of the local partnership, there is a high probability a crosswalk analysis between the former state standards and the Common Core already exists and is available as a valuable resource for local vertical teams to use to understand the difference between previous and current standards. The type of analysis described later is a gap analysis identifying which knowledge and skills are currently being taught versus what needs to be taught as required by state standards and local priorities.

2. *Standard to assessment alignment* refers to an analysis examining the relationship between the standards and all forms of assessment. Overall, the purpose is to ensure that the various assessments provide reliable measures of the standards. Researchers have developed many ways to analyze standards and assessments, varying in complexity from simple content matches to explorations of rigor and cognitive demand. Local educators can review (so they do not have

to recreate) the psychometric analysis of any statewide or nationally developed assessments. For example, there is extensive field-testing and research currently being conducted by the two common assessment consortiums developing the Common Core assessments. To review the research, go to the website for the Partnership for Assessment of Readiness for College and Careers (www.parcconline .org/assessment-research) or the Smarter Balanced Assessment Consortium (www.smarterbalanced.org/smarter-balanced-assess ments/item-writing-and-review/). Local assessments experts, however, should be called on to examine any locally developed assessments (such as local placement exams) to determine the relationship between what is being taught and what is being assessed to ensure what is being measured accurately reflects what knowledge and skills students need to be successful.

3. *Standard to curriculum alignment* refers to matching the standards to the curriculum being taught. Curriculum is the explicit plan for what content will be taught. The purpose of aligning the college and career readiness standards such as the Common Core to curriculum is to ensure students will have the opportunity to learn the ELA and mathematics knowledge and skills they need to be postsecondary ready. This type of alignment is the focus of the process for this chapter. Identifying the gaps between what is currently taught and what the standards require helps define the curriculum development work to be addressed by the vertical teams. This analysis provides a key opportunity to look at curriculum both vertically and horizontally to determine that all students, regardless of what course or instructor they take, will have access to a fully articulated and aligned curriculum. For the purpose of the book, educators are asked to think of curriculum along a secondary to postsecondary continuum, not in isolation by grade level, course title, or educational level.

4. *Standard to practice alignment* refers to analyzing the standards in relation to current instructional practice. Instructional practice is how teachers engage the students with the standards. The purpose is to understand the relationship of the standards to how that content is being taught and learned in the classroom. Whereas the state standards (such as the Common Core) offer a clear target for assessment development and curriculum planning, as stated in Chapter 1, the standards do not identify how teachers should teach. The responsibility for how to best teach the college and career readiness standards ultimately lies with local educators.

Curriculum and instructional practice are interrelated, representing "the what and the how" of teaching and learning. Standard to practice alignment requires educators to think differently about their instruction by planning activities and incorporating various instructional techniques to teach the new standards. For example, the Common Core represent a significant departure from the preexisting standards in most states. The teachers convened by the Illinois State Board of Education (ISBE) found that the new standards were more clearly stated and focused with increased depth and rigor (see www .isbe.net/common_core/pdf/gap_analysis_intro.pdf). Simply taking a procedural or checklist approach to implementing the new standards, while maintaining previous practice, will leave students unprepared for the increased expectations.

For this book, the standard to practice alignment work then becomes part of the ongoing sustainability of the partnership. The remainder of this chapter describes how to create a curriculum aligned to a college and career readiness trajectory. Once the curriculum is created, the vertical teamwork is ongoing. The vertical teams then meet at least annually not only to refine the aligned curriculum but to share best practices and the most effective strategies for how to teach the curriculum. This can include the sharing of assignments, assessments, and peer visits to each other's classes. Ultimately, the work should become ingrained in the ongoing curricular and instructional work at the participating educational institutions, and the vertical teams can be powerful professional learning communities to increase the college and career readiness for all students.

Aligning Standards to Curriculum

Once the vertical teams are convened and are on the same page about creating an aligned curriculum, they can move on to the collaborative processes of integrating the desired college and career readiness standards and then aligning curricula to college and career readiness expectations. These are ongoing and iterative processes. Based on existing research and EPIC's alignment work around the country, this section outlines a five-step process to align curricula to standards:

Step 1: Share Existing Curriculum

Step 2: Conduct a Gap Analysis

Step 3: Align Content

Step 4: Calibrate Student Performance Expectations

Step 5: Direct Ongoing Efforts

An important consideration before undertaking this work is that this process requires time for meeting both internally (faculty meetings for individual departments) and externally (vertical team meetings with shared subject area faculty members across institutions) and also time for faculty members to conduct independent work. Therefore, the creation of a successful college and career readiness curriculum requires external support in two ways. First, leadership must be provided to schedule, facilitate, and organize the work. Second, faculty members must be provided time to do the work. A key priority for the executive leadership team overseeing the entire local postsecondary partnership is to ascertain the resources to provide leadership and time for the faculty members to participate in this critical endeavor, reducing the chasm between secondary and postsecondary readiness. The description of the five-step process that follows assumes that the executive leadership team, including support from school districts and postsecondary institutions, has provided these requisite resources for the participating faculty members to successfully engage in the work.

Step 1: Share Existing Curricula

The first step in aligning curricula to a college and career readiness trajectory is to have documented curricula that can be shared. Existing curricular materials should then be collected from all participating faculty members (high school and postsecondary). The purpose of collecting this information is to have a starting point for the analyses. Identifying current course content is a prerequisite for being able to determine how the content relates to the college and career readiness standards and who is teaching what content. Curriculum refers to an explicit plan regarding what content will be taught. For postsecondary faculty, traditionally this curriculum documentation is in the format of a course syllabus. For high school faculty, the format of curricula typically has greater variance, ranging from a formal district- or school-written curricula or pacing guides to more informal, individually developed, lesson plans.

> Identifying current course content is a prerequisite for being able to determine how the content relates to the college and career readiness standards and who is teaching what content.

The transparency of sharing curricula among high school and entry-level college instructors allows for greater insight into the content, sequencing, pacing, rigor, and expectations of courses at both levels. Accompanying documents such as student assignments, assessments, work samples, and grading rubrics helpfully illustrate course content, enabling participants to conduct more comprehensive alignment analyses. After existing curricula are documented and collected, all curricular materials can be analyzed and explicitly aligned to the desired standards and learning objectives (following the process described in subsequent steps). Partnership members can then identify student work and other supporting materials that illustrate what college and career readiness looks like in practice. Once this process is complete, departments can analyze course sequences and student performance expectations to determine horizontal and vertical alignment. The result is more transparent, standards-based course development, and a documented system that allows for ongoing review and improvement.

Recommended Tool/Strategy:
Develop and Maintain Detailed Course Syllabi

Accomplishing the first step in sharing existing curriculum varies in the length of time necessary to complete it. In EPIC's experiences working with vertical teams, postsecondary education faculty members typically have well-documented curricula readily available in the form of a syllabus. Having readily available curricula has not been the case within high schools. Many high school faculty members have not historically been asked to provide formally documented curriculum and will require additional time and possibly guidance on how to document the curriculum in a useful manner. EPIC staff has spent considerable time assisting high school faculty members in creating high quality syllabi aligned to required standards. The following section provides an example of how this work might be approached.

One tool that is useful to the process of documenting curriculum is a detailed course syllabus. When properly developed and maintained, a syllabus communicates to students, parents, administrators, and other instructors a set of highly relevant details that can be used to improve both horizontal and vertical alignment of content knowledge and student expectations. Benefits of using syllabi include the following:

- Consolidating the most information about a course into a single document
- Familiarizing students with a document used by postsecondary institutions to help better prepare them for college and career readiness
- Increasing student and parent understanding of course content and expectations
- Encouraging collaboration among instructors, providing a professional development experience to create and compare course content, and receiving feedback about the syllabi
- Providing an efficient and consistent way to gather information on an institution's curriculum

Using a common format for all instructors (ideally across high school and college) is one strategy for streamlining curriculum alignment. These documents significantly simplify the process of comparing syllabi and mapping course content to college and career readiness standards, making them the building blocks for a curriculum aligned to aspects of college and career readiness. A common format should include the following features:

a. Course objectives

b. Prerequisite knowledge and skills necessary for success

c. Required texts

d. Teaching methods employed

e. Course schedule

f. Unit descriptions broken down by topics and activities

g. Standards (targeted college and career readiness standards, such as the Common Core, plus other standards, such as science, CTE, fine arts, etc.) addressed in each unit

h. In-class and homework assignments for each unit and their weight relative to course grade

i. Assessments planned for each unit and their weight relative to course grade

j. Classroom policies

k. Grading policies

Figure 6.1 demonstrates an example of a high quality syllabus. A blank syllabus template that instructors can use for creating standardized syllabi can be downloaded for free at www.epiconline.org/illinois_templates.

EPIC has developed CourseCreate, an online system for generating high quality syllabi consistently across a department or institution. The system enables educators to create a detailed course syllabus and electronically select the Common Core taught within the course. Instructors who complete CourseCreate can generate a PDF or HTML file of the syllabus for downloading, posting, and sharing. The system then serves as an online repository of course syllabi, allowing instructors to share, comment, and edit each other's work if desired. In addition, the syllabi created through this process can immediately be analyzed against the Common Core, generating a curriculum map (CoursePathway) of who is teaching what standard in what course (for more information, please visit collegeready.epiconline.org/info/create.dot).

Figure 6.1   English 11 Course Sample Syllabus

This syllabus clearly communicates expectations to students and contains enough detail to be used effectively in both vertical and horizontal alignment efforts.

Teacher: Jane Smith

Classroom: 204

Available after school: 3–4 PM, M, W, Th

About This Course

This course is an in-depth study of pieces of world literature. It includes a variety of genres in a chronological sequence. There is a strong emphasis on writing and critical analysis of the texts.

This course is aligned to the Common Core State Standards in English Language Arts.

Assignment Policies

Assignments are due at the beginning of class. Include your full name, the course name, period number, and the assignment title.

Grading Policies

A: 94–100	C: 74–79
A-: 90–93	C-: 70–73
B: 84–89	F: 0–69
B-: 81–83	

Attendance Policy

Daily attendance means coming to class on time and being prepared for the lesson. For excused absences, doctor's notes must be provided to the main office and must include the doctor's office number.

❄ ❄

Curriculum and Course Schedule

Topic 1: Hamlet—Journal

Standards:

A. Range of Reading and Level of Text Complexity: Read and comprehend literature. [RL.11-12.10]

B. Range of Writing: Write routinely over shorter time frames. [W.11-12.10]

Assignment: Reading Journal

Students will keep a journal while reading Hamlet, answering a prompt the teacher has provided for each reading assignment and including their own observations about the text. This journal will form the basis of class discussions.

Topic 2: Hamlet—Language

Standards:

A. Craft and Structure: Determine the meanings of words and phrases. [RL.11-12.4]

B. Craft and Structure: Analyze the impact of specific words. [RL.11-12.4]

Assignment: Analyzing Language

Students will discuss an assigned passage from Hamlet, which analyzes the passage for use of language including: (a) the meanings of important words, both connotative and denotative; (b) the possible meanings of figurative language; (c) how the language choices affect meaning; how interpretations of the meaning of the passage change, depending on how the word is defined or depending on the figure of speech; (d) how the language choices affect tone. Does the tone change based on the definition of the word or the interpretation of the figure of speech?

(Continued)

(Continued)

Students will discuss why William Shakespeare might have chosen a particular word and why he included a particular figure of speech. Results of the discussion will be synthesized in a paper.

Topic 3: Hamlet—Themes

Standards:

A. Key Ideas and Details: Determine themes or central ideas. [RL.11-12.2]

B. Range of Writing: Write routinely over extended time frames. [W.11-12.10]

C. Research to Build and Present Knowledge: Apply reading standards to literature. [W.11-12.9a]

Assignment: *Theme Essay*

Students will analyze Hamlet and be able to identify, in writing, two major themes. Students will provide multiple examples from the text to support each theme statement. The essay will focus on how these themes interact with and build on each other. In the course of their essay, they should provide multiple examples from the text to support each theme statement. They should note how William Shakespeare orders the details he reveals (e.g., why he has the ghost appear at the start of the play).

Step 2: Conduct a Gap Analysis

The next step in curriculum alignment is to identify the college and career readiness standards that are present, duplicated, and missing in the existing curriculum. This is called a gap analysis. After determining where duplication and gaps exist, planning for addressing these issues can begin. This section outlines a four-step approach to conducting a gap analysis. Several steps reference example templates for organizing the information recorded and discussed during the process of conducting a gap analysis. Blank versions of these templates and templates prepopulated with the Common Core can be downloaded for free at www.epiconline.org/illinois_templates.

1. *Review and understand the targeted standards (such as the Common Core).*

Educators who are familiar with the structure and content of the targeted standards, such as the Common Core, will be better equipped to identify how the content they are already teaching aligns to these new expectations. Information about the Common Core can be located and the standards downloaded here: www.corestandards.org. Participants should consider the following recommendations when reviewing the Common Core:

Process for Conducting a Gap Analysis:

1. Review and understand the targeted standards (such as the Common Core).

2. Map the targeted standards to the existing curriculum documents.

3. Determine the degree of alignment between the targeted standards and the existing curriculum.

4. List the missing targeted standards.

Note: Individual educators should follow this process in preparation for the collaborative work outlined in the preceding sections for Steps 3, 4, and 5. It should also be noted that the process documented here is a manual alternative to the process automated by the CourseCreate tool, described in Step 1 (p. 88).

- Become familiar with how the standards are organized. The organization varies by subject area and grade level.
- Review the relevant grade-level standards in the desired subject area. Postsecondary ELA faculty would review the standards in the 11–12 grade bands. Postsecondary mathematics faculty would review the standards in the high school conceptual themes. All faculty in all subject areas should read and review the Reading Standards for Literacy in History/Social Studies and Science and Technical Subjects, the College and Career Readiness Anchor Standards for Writing, and the Writing Standards for Literacy in History/Social Studies, Science, and Technical Subjects.
- Review appendices for exemplars, sample text complexity, and sample performance tasks.
- Examine how standards progress over the grade levels. Determine what is implied in one grade span because it is previously articulated in another, note when redundancy is assumed and not stated, and determine the significance of a redundancy.

2. *Map the targeted standards to the existing curriculum documents.*

Using the gap analysis tool illustrated in Table 6.1, begin the analysis of the existing curriculum in relation to the targeted standards. At this point in the process, faculty members are working independently to identify which standards are being taught in their individual courses. Faculty members review each of the targeted standards (i.e., Common Core) listed in Column A and its location within the curriculum noted in Column B (such as unit, topic, or page number, depending on how the curriculum is organized). Educators should consider the course themes, units of study, and essential questions addressed by the course as currently taught when selecting which Common Core are represented in the curriculum. A gap analysis tool prepopulated with the Common Core in Column A can be downloaded from www.epiconline.org/illinois_templates.

Optional: If the course curriculum is already mapped to the previous standards, the existing crosswalk document can be used to assist in the process of selecting which targeted standards should be mapped to the curriculum. Using the prepopulated standards in Column A, insert a new Column B with a header, "Previous Standards." Educators can fill in Column B with previous state standards that have been matched to the Common Core in the crosswalk. They will then be able to easily identify which of the targeted standards are not addressed in their course; they can then skip the next step and place an X in the last column identifying the targeted standards that are not addressed. Please note that in some cases, multiple standards will align to a single targeted standard. Therefore, multiple standards can be entered in the same cell in the corresponding row to the applicable targeted standard. If the curriculum map is already available, this saves a step for each faculty member having to identify which Common Core are being addressed in each course.

Table 6.1   Example of Gap Analysis Tool Headers

A	B	C	D	E
Targeted Standards (i.e., Common Core)	Location Within the Curriculum (unit, page number, etc.)	Match/ No Match/ Partial Match	Explanatory Notes Regarding Match Determination	Missing Standards (mark with an X)

3. *Determine the degree of alignment between the target standards and the existing curriculum.*

Once Column B, the "Location Within the Curriculum" (unit, page number, etc.), is completed, the relationship between the targeted standard and the specific content being taught should be analyzed. Examining the Common Core in the context of specific curricular elements (units, activities, etc.) enables educators to think about the level of detail or degree of coverage addressed in the curriculum as currently designed. Educators make a determination in Column C of whether each targeted standard is fully matched, partially matched, or not matched to the curriculum:

- *Match:* Curriculum addresses the depth and coverage of the standard as written.
- *Partial Match:* Curriculum partially addresses the standard but does not fully match the depth and coverage as written.
- *No Match:* Curriculum does not address the standard.

Please note that many standards are written to be multiple-barreled, meaning that a single standard statement may contain several different concepts. For example, a double-barreled standard is one that states, "Students must be able to add and subtract double digits." When only one or more of the concepts, but not all contained in the standard, are addressed in a course, a partial match is selected. Therefore, a partial match would occur if there is only a match with addition and not subtraction, or vice versa. Column D is then used to annotate what is missing for a partial match decision.

4. *List the missing targeted standards.*

After noting the degree of alignment between the targeted standards and the existing curriculum, educators can make note of which standards do not appear in the course by placing an X in Column E whenever there is a no match identified in Column C. The spreadsheet can then be sorted by Column E, and all of the targeted standards with no match are identified. In addition, the content identified in the explanatory notes in Column D is also added to the list of standards not addressed in that course.

Please note that no single course would necessarily be expected to address every targeted standard. The intent is for instructors to identify which subset of standards is being addressed in individual courses, with the idea in the preceding Step 3 that all instructors within a department, and then eventually across institutions, would examine a sequence (pathway) of courses to determine if all standards are being taught among a combination of courses.

Overall, engaging in the process of considering (a) which targeted standards are not present in the curriculum and (b) areas where the degree of match between the targeted standards and the curriculum is only partial (meaning that the standard would not be adequately addressed currently) reveals the "gaps" that are addressed in the preceding Step 3. Conversely, noting which targeted standards are addressed repeatedly within a single course or among a combination of courses along a typical course pathway identifies the duplication that also needs to be considered.

Step 3: Align Content

This stage of the standards to curriculum alignment process involves revising curricula to be vertically and horizontally aligned to the targeted college and career readiness standards. The prior steps enabled educators to understand what they are currently teaching in relation to the targeted standards. This step enables educators to collaborate about who should be teaching what and which changes need to be made to existing curricula to achieve seamless alignment.

This is a multifaceted process that involves facilitating the work across individuals, course titles, course pathways, and educational systems/institutions. Ideally, department heads and instructional leaders from participating institutions would meet to map out the time lines for each of the steps described here so that the individual and institution-specific work can be completed concurrently to enable all parties to be in similar stages of development when interorganizational collaboration is needed.

Process for Content Alignment

A. Review individually the results of the gap analysis.

B. Convene subject area teams within an institution.

C. Convene subject area vertical teams.

D. Revise curriculum to align to the targeted college and career readiness standards.

A. *Review individually the results of the gap analysis.*

Faculty members should review the results of their individual gap analyses, clearly identify which target standards are being taught in each individual's course, and more importantly, check to make sure that the course provides sufficient opportunities for students to learn and demonstrate the designated content.

B. *Convene subject area teams within an institution.*

While the ultimate goal is to work collaboratively between secondary and postsecondary institutions, an important step before that vertical collaboration is to have faculty members within a high school and within a college meet separately (within their school/college, not across education systems) to agree on what content should be taught within a similar course title and between the sequence of courses in that subject area. This is a particularly important conversation for faculty members who teach the same course but might not have previously collaborated to reach agreement on which content should be taught in the course.

Participating faculty members should bring their individual work from the gap analysis described in Step A for comparison. The subject area teams need to agree on what standards should be taught in what courses, both horizontally and vertically. The faculty members teaching the same course should work together to reach horizontal agreement, meaning that all faculty members teaching the same class should agree on similar content (although the instructional plans, activities, and assessments may vary). Once consensus has been reached on the content of individual courses, subject area departments need to reach vertical agreement, meaning that the department should determine the correct sequencing of content and address duplication and omissions of standards across the sequence of courses. Faculty should consider the prerequisite and subsequent courses and course themes and/or essential questions and identify the standards that should be addressed throughout the sequence of courses. Students learn and retain best when the standards are sequenced in a way that builds on student knowledge and skills throughout the subject area course pathway.

The gap analysis tool can also be expanded to include columns indicating what courses are teaching what standards. This tool then becomes a de facto curriculum map that visually represents the sequence of what standards are being taught over a course pathway. For an example of what this could look like, Figure 6.2 offers

Figure 6.2   Example of a Curriculum Map Using CourseCreate

 Cource**Pathway**™

Pathway Analysis

Standards

● All Components Submitted   ◑ One or More Components Submitted

Common Core English Language Arts 11-12

	Pathway Confirmed	11th Grade English *Gunther Fritz*	12th Grade English *Rutherford Bee*
1. Cite strong and thorough textual evidence to support analysis of what the text says explicitly as well as inferences drawn from text, in . . .	●	●	●
2. Determine two or more themes or central ideas of a text and analyze their development over the course of the text, including how they intera . . .	●	●	
3. Analyze the impact of the author's choices regarding how to develop and relate elements of a story or drama (e.g., where a story is set, how . . .	●	◑	◑
4. Determine the meaning of words and phrases as they are used in the text, including figurative and connotative meanings; analyze the impact o . . .	●	◑	◑
5. Analyze how an author's choices concerning how to structure specific parts of a text (e.g., the choice of where to begin or end a story, the . . .	●		●
6. Analyze a case in which grasping point of view requires distinguishing what is directly stated in a text from what is really meant (e.g., sa . . .			
7. Analyze multiple interpretations of a story, drama, or poem (e.g., recorded or live production of a play or recorded novel or poetry), evalu . . .			
8. Demonstrate knowledge of eighteenth-, nineteenth- and early-twentieth-century foundational works of American literature, including how two o . . .	●	●	
9. By the end of grade 11, read and comprehend, literature, including stories, dramas, and poems, in the grades 11-CCR text complexity band pro . . .			

Source: McGaughy, C., van der Valk, A., Singleton, J., Zalewski, T., & Farkas, R. (2012).

a visual representation of an automated curriculum map, called CoursePathway, generated by the CourseCreate system described earlier in this chapter (please note that the teachers' names under each course title are not real and are included as examples.).

C. *Convene subject area vertical teams.*

The next step in the process is to convene the vertical teams, including the subject area faculty members from participating high schools and colleges. The process for aligning curriculum vertically across educational levels should mirror the process for reaching internal agreement detailed in the previous section. After various partner institutions reach internal agreement on course content, vertical teams should meet to align the courses across institutions. Ideally, postsecondary faculty members within a department teaching entry-level courses would meet with their high school faculty counterparts from feeder districts. In large areas with multiple school districts and high schools, subject area vertical teams can be convened with representatives from the various institutions. These representatives not only work to reach consensus about seamless alignment between courses, they also serve as instructional leaders to share findings and collect input and feedback from their colleagues back at their campus.

D. *Revise curriculum to align to the targeted college and career readiness standards.*

Once faculty across institutions agree on what should be taught in each course, faculty members should revise curriculum accordingly to ensure that students are provided the opportunity to learn the agreed on content. If faculty members need support in refining their curriculum, local experts should be utilized to provide professional development. The experts could be professional development providers from a regional educational service center, curriculum specialists

---

Critical Questions to Guide Content Alignment Conversations:

Which standards are being taught in which courses?

1. When standards are duplicated across a course sequence, is this intentional? Is it repetitive? Is it building on prior learning to increase rigor and depth of understanding?

2. When standards are missing, is that intentional? When should those standards be addressed?

3. When courses are only partially addressing a standard, is the missing part(s) taught in another course? What additional content should be added to which course to completely address the standard?

from participating school districts, or they could be recruited from a college of education. The ultimate goal is a fully articulated curriculum aligned to the targeted standards for all of the students within the institution of higher education's feeder pattern.

Step 4: Align Student Performance Expectations

In addition to aligning content, expectations for student performance also need to be calibrated. As Conley (2010) noted, "One of the most traumatic experiences first-year college students encounter is the deference in instructor expectations on exams and papers between high school and college courses" (p. 121). Frequently, instructors at both the high school and college levels assess student work in isolation, largely relying on personal experience as the reference point. This leads to the misalignment of performance expectations at three levels:

- *Instructor to instructor:* Are some instructors more demanding and some more lenient in the challenge level and grading practices for student work?
- *Campus to campus:* Does a course offered at one campus require a comparable level of rigor as the same course at another campus? Is an A at one educational institution equivalent to an A at another?
- *Secondary to postsecondary:* Does a student have to demonstrate the same level of cognitive demand for the same content in high school as in college? Would a 12th-grade student receive the same grade on the same assignment in a high school course versus an entry-level college course?

The purpose of Step 4 is to improve the clarity and consistency of expectations of secondary and postsecondary faculty members to ensure students are prepared for the rigor of postsecondary work. This chapter describes two ways to approach the calibration: first, by considering the cognitive demand (challenge level) of what is being taught, and second, by creating shared rubrics and exemplars clearly illustrating expectations for student performance.

Assessing the Cognitive Demand

There is increasing pressure for students to demonstrate their knowledge and skills in increasingly complex ways to be prepared for postsecondary success by the time they leave high school. In addition to the content review described in Steps 1 to 3, educators should spend time reviewing curriculum activities to identify the levels of challenge and cognitive demand students are asked to meet. **By engaging in this step of the alignment process, educators will confirm that they are not only teaching progressively sequenced content but providing sufficient rigor for students to graduate high school prepared for the challenge level they will encounter in their postsecondary learning environments.** Once the content review is complete, instructors should then consider the rigor (cognitive demand) of the curriculum. Facilitators can work with the vertical teams to assist them in assessing the cognitive demand of what they intend to teach to ensure sufficient rigor.

The term "rigor" is ubiquitous in educational jargon but very subjective. For this book, rigor refers to the cognitive complexity of how a student is expected to interact with the required content (harkening back to Bloom's taxonomy). In working with educators to develop curriculum aligned to a college and career readiness trajectory, EPIC uses a modified version of Webb's (1997) seminal alignment work defining the depth of knowledge (DOK). This approach analyzes performance expectations by considering the "number of ideas integrated, depth of reasoning required, knowledge transferred to new situations, multiple forms of representation employed, and mental effort sustained" (Webb, 1997, p. 17). Cognitive complexity, as represented by the DOK rating scale described in Table 6.2, represents the challenge level of the interaction with the content within a standard, ranging on a four-point scale from *recall* to *extended thinking* (adapted from Conley et al., 2011a).

The process for working with vertical teams in assessing the cognitive demand of their curriculum involves having participants analyze the major activities, assignments, and assessments included in their courses. Suggested steps for these meetings are as follows:

1. To begin, have participating faculty members bring their final projects or final examinations to share.

2. Have the faculty members become familiar with the purpose of assessing the cognitive demand and the DOK rating scale and examples provided in Table 6.2. Additional resources can be found at the Wisconsin Center of Education Research website (www.wcer.wisc.edu/WAT/index.aspx).

3. Have the group reach consensus about the desired DOK level for each project or examination. If using the Common Core, provide the vertical team Appendix B from the Lining Up report (Conley et al., 2011b). Appendix B lists the DOK level of each targeted standard. This is important to note because the goal is not to reach a Level 4 on every assignment. The Common Core represents a college and career readiness trajectory, which varies

in range for each individual standard from 1 to 4. Tables 6.3 and 6.4 show the overall distribution of the DOK levels for the Common Core in ELA and for math, respectively (Conley et al., 2011b, pp. 16, 22).

Table 6.2   Depth of Knowledge Rating Scale

DOK Level	Description	Examples
Level 1 Recall	Recall of a fact, information, or procedure	ELA: Recall elements and details of story structure, such as sequence of events, character, plot, and setting. Math: Compute with numbers (i.e., add, subtract, multiply, divide).
Level 2 Skills/ Concepts	Use of information or conceptual knowledge (including more than one step) and engagement of some mental processing beyond a habitual response	ELA: Identify cause and effect, and understand the main idea and purpose implied by the text. Math: Solve two-step linear equations and inequalities in one variable over the rational numbers, interpret the solution or solutions in the context from which they arose, and verify the reasonableness of results.
Level 3 Strategic Thinking	Requires reasoning, a developing plan, or a sequence of steps, with a task with some complexity and more than one possible answer	ELA: Evaluate the relative accuracy and usefulness of information from different sources. Math: Understand solving equations as a process of reasoning and explain the reasoning.
Level 4 Extended Thinking	Requires an investigation, time to think and process multiple conditions of an open-ended problem, and the synthesis of data or information	ELA: Locate, gather, analyze, and evaluate written information for the purpose of drafting a reasoned report that supports and appropriately illustrates references and conclusions drawn from research. Math: Design a statistical experiment to study a problem and communicate the outcomes.

Source: McGaughy, C., van der Valk, A., Singleton, J., Zalewski, T., & Farkas, R. (2012).

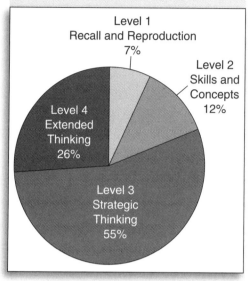

Table 6.3 DOK Levels of Common Core ELA Standards

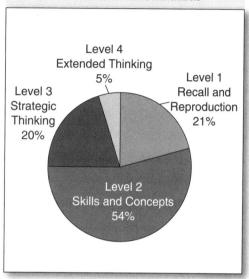

Table 6.4 DOK Levels of Common Core Math Standards

Source: Conley, D. T., Drummond, K., DeGonzalez, A., Seburn, M., Stout, O., & Rooseboom, J. (2011).

It is critical for faculty members to develop, jointly (across a department and between high school and college), a sequence of activities and assignments that culminates at the college and career level by the end of high school. They need to reach agreement on what DOK level students need to be able to demonstrate in each exit-level high school course to be prepared for the subsequent entry-level postsecondary course. They then need to backward map (reverse design from Grade 12 down to elementary) the challenge level of the student performance expectations down to the lower grades to create a seamless progression so students will reach the college and career readiness target. All culminating activities, assignments, and assessments that do not meet the desired DOK level should then be revised to be at the desired level of rigor.

Sample Assignment
Demonstrating Increasing Rigor

Lower challenge level:

Students select 5 sources from a list of 20 provided by the teacher on the subject of bee colony collapse. Based on the evidence contained within these sources, students summarize competing views regarding this phenomenon. Students correctly cite each source and provide a correctly formatted bibliography.

(Continued)

(Continued)

Medium challenge level:

Students independently research bee colony collapse and develop an annotated bibliography of five sources they believe to be objective and credible. Based on the evidence contained within these sources, students write a paper summarizing competing views regarding this phenomenon and propose a strategy to prevent further collapse. Students correctly cite each source and provide a correctly formatted bibliography, including their descriptions of why each source provides valid, scientific, evidence.

Higher challenge level:

Students listen to an invited guest speaker—such as a local biologist. During the presentation, the biologist discusses endangered animal species and the implications of losing these animals from their ecosystems. Examples include bat populations that are being decimated by white-nose syndrome and bees that are disappearing due to colony collapse disorder. In both of these cases, scientists are struggling to understand the problems that these populations face.

This biologist poses a research challenge for the class: Select an endangered animal, conduct research on this animal population, and create a presentation that explains the threats facing the animal and the animal's ecosystem. The presentation should include the following:

- Identify the causes of the animal population decline as they are currently understood. The causes of the decline may be natural or man-made.
- Predict local and global consequences if this trend of population decline isn't reversed.
- Analyze current solutions for the problem and propose additional ways for humans to intervene and reverse the current trends. Evaluate possible interventions as to their feasibility, cost, and likeliness to succeed.
- Include a map of the global population of the animal you chose. Illustrate how the animal population's reach has changed over time.

Creating Shared Rubrics and Exemplars

Developing shared rubrics with exemplars of student work provides reference points for grading of student work that involve subjective evaluations. Evaluating student work is a particularly complex and challenging task for educators due to the reliance on professional judgment, experience, and variance in curriculum. Engaging in a shared scoring process helps reduce the variance in performance expectations by creating a shared mental model for scoring evidence of student learning. Often the process includes scoring a variety of documents in collaboration with secondary and postsecondary colleagues, allowing the group to come to agreement about what constitutes evidence of successful student performance. Increasing the consistency and transparency of student performance expectations improves the development and selection of curricular activities that will prepare students to meet them.

No vertical team should have to start from scratch in developing a rubric. There are multiple options in making the process more efficient. First, scoring rubrics are ubiquitous in the educational arena. Many high schools and colleges have already adopted the schoolwide use of some rubrics. Ask participating faculty members to bring existing rubrics to the vertical team meeting, and work with the group to review, discuss, and reach consensus on what rubric to use or revise. If a locally developed rubric does not suffice, there are vast resources available online at no charge. The facilitator or vertical team leaders can download some sample rubrics off the Internet for the vertical team to review, discuss, and revise. For rubrics assessing the Common Core, the states receiving federal Race to the Top funding have created significant materials (for example, Delaware and Tennessee were first-round winners and have extensive materials available on their state education websites). National organizations, such as the Literacy Design Collaborative (ldc.org) and the Mathematics Assessment Project (map.mathshell.org) have task banks and rubrics available to assist instructors in assessing the Common Core. Finally, if the vertical team wants to develop its own rubrics, there are free online tools that enable instructors to create high quality rubrics (see, e.g., RubiStar at rubistar.4teachers.org).

Once a rubric has been selected, faculty members should provide prompts and student work samples representing a variety of abilities (Remember to gain necessary consents and remove all identifying information.). The group first scores each sample using a common scoring rubric and then ranks them in order of proficiency. The group facilitator averages the rankings and the group discusses them. The facilitator should prompt the group to consider the following questions:

- What influenced the scoring decisions?
- What evidence did a student need to provide to prompt various scoring decisions?
- What were some of the key performance indicators that emerged as decision points between higher and lower scores?

Finally, the group can use this reflection and discussion to establish benchmark levels and agreed on scoring standards that can be shared and used to gauge student growth over time. These agreements should be documented for future use in two ways: first, by revising the rubric to ensure that the scoring level indicators are clearly described, and second, by identifying student work samples representing each scoring level on the rubric. The work samples should be clearly annotated with the rationale as to why the student work sample was scored at that level. These resources should then be used at each institution. The vertical team members can then serve as the trainers back in their home department to support their colleagues in implementing the shared scoring rubrics. These types of group scoring sessions can then occur regularly throughout and beyond the curriculum alignment process as part of ongoing professional development.

Critical Reflection Questions

By the end of this stage, the educators should work to ensure their curriculum and expectations follow a logical progression. Teachers may have to recalibrate some of their curriculum to fit within the vertical sequence and properly fit within the learning continuum. Educators should analyze their activities vertically by course sequence. Participants should periodically reflect on and address the following questions:

- Are there opportunities for students to engage in a wide variety of curriculum activities to prepare them for the range of activities at the postsecondary level?
- Do students have increasing responsibility and independence when demonstrating their learning?
- Do the activities from course to course progress in challenge levels and cognitive demand, culminating at the college and career readiness level?
- Is duplication purposeful or redundant?

Step 5: Direct Ongoing Efforts

This chapter has described a process for standards to curriculum alignment. This is an ongoing, iterative process that does not stop after the initial work is completed. After this initial vertical and horizontal alignment process, ongoing moderation and calibration of student performance expectations will help to continually maintain and improve curriculum alignment. Examples of the ongoing vertical team activities include the following:

- Conducting peer-to-peer classroom visits to the high schools and colleges.
- Analyzing any new state-required summative assessments (such as PARCC or the Smarter Balanced Assessment Consortium [SBAC] assessments states are implementing to assess the Common Core). This analysis should include reviewing what will be assessed and if the curriculum needs to be revised to better prepare students to succeed on these new assessments.
- Calibrating scoring expectations by participating in annual norming sessions to examine and grade student work samples in vertical teams.
- Monitoring postsecondary success indicators such as decreased remedial/development education placements, higher entry-level college course grades, and increased student retention and graduation rates.
- Participating in ongoing curriculum and course planning across levels.
- Sharing best-practice activities, assignments, assessments, and placement exams across levels.
- Troubleshooting as a group any particularly challenging concepts or lessons to teach.

Ultimately, vertical teaming should become part of the curriculum and instructional practice embedded in the local region. Over time, strong relationships and institutional commitments should sustain the work, resulting in a seamless academic transition for students from high school to their postsecondary learning environment.

SUMMARY

This chapter describes how local partnerships can align curricula across educational systems. This process of connecting curricula involves teams of educators working together to examine and refine what is being taught and to build learning pathways for each successive year of education—culminating with students arriving at their desired postsecondary institution prepared to succeed in entry-level coursework. This chapter provides both an overview of alignment work and a "how-to" guide for local teams of high school and college instructors to partner to align their curriculum.

DISCUSSION QUESTIONS

- What are the biggest gaps in preparation your students face when entering college and careers?
- In which subject would your partnership wish to start alignment work? Will you focus on core academics, applied/integrated pathways, or another option?
- Does your partnership have existing vertical teams? If not, are there any barriers to developing such teams?
- How will your vertical team members reach agreement about which content and level of expectations should be taught?

Supporting and Sustaining Partnerships

First and foremost, the work of partnerships is about building and sustaining relationships and trust; relationships across systems have few incentives to develop, scarce resources, layers of politics, and deep historical disconnects. In recent years, the constant churn of the education policy "du jour" has created an environment in which leaders and their staff come and go, making it challenging to forge lasting relationships. Politics within and between people, educational systems, and individual schools and postsecondary institutions can easily derail the best laid plans. Getting beyond politics is particularly difficult, since our educational systems developed separately and have different goals, objectives, and incentives related to key organizational missions and areas such as funding, pedagogy, accountability, professional development, assessment, curriculum development and expectations, and other key issues. Yet students are directly affected by disconnects in those areas as they traverse from one system to another.

The partnerships that have sustained these efforts—in Long Beach, California (www.longbeachcollegepromise.org), and El Paso, Texas (www.epcae.org), for example—usually have trusted, well-respected leaders, who stay in their positions, or at least in positions of influence within the region, for a long time. The tools in this book will help both experienced and new partnerships with their work, but the trust building needs to be done carefully, strategically, and over time. Thus, to be most successful, the tools and strategies need to be used in environments in which the relationships are on solid footing, with agreement on key goals and objectives.

Predictable Barriers to Success

There are multiple barriers and potential land mines in navigating partnerships. In the field of community development, collaboration can be viewed as a continuum among *compliance, cooperation,* and full *collaboration.* Compliance refers to doing what the head of a system or educational entity tells a person or group to do, but there is no buy-in behind compliance. Often, the opposite can occur. People can comply outwardly but act in ways behind the scenes that can be detrimental for the success of the initiative at hand. Cooperation refers to the increased involvement, investment, and attention to shared goals (this is a form of "parallel programming," akin to parallel play); collaboration refers to interagency policymaking and resource and service integration ("integrative programming"; Crowson & Boyd, 1996).

The different approaches have trade-offs. Parallel programming "experiences fewer administrative problems such as turfism, facilities management, personnel policies, planning, professional preparation, communication, confidentiality, and information retrieval" (Smrekar & Mawhinney, 1999, p. 447). Integrative programming, by definition, reshapes institutional authority and practice and challenges entrenched authority. Such efforts require well-established trust and community consensus (Crowson & Boyd, 1996). Therefore, at the early stages of any partnership, cooperation is the goal. To avoid derailing the process, true collaboration should only occur as a natural outgrowth of cooperation when all parties see the need for deep integration.

> To avoid derailing the process, true collaboration should only occur as a natural outgrowth of cooperation when all parties see the need for deep integration.

Even well-planned collaborations often encounter daunting challenges around engagement, sustainability, and logistics when convened (Sambolt & Balestreri, 2013).

Specifically, some of the land mines include the following:

- Too few, too many, or not the right people at the table
- The wrong leadership
- Major disagreements that are not settled (often these might have historical roots and could have started under different leaders)

- An agenda that is either too broad or too vague or difficulty agreeing on an agenda
- No understanding of where the other partners are coming from.
- No perspective that "we're all in this together"
- No specific, measurable goals or no mechanism to measure progress or hold individuals accountable
- Lack of resources, funding, and staff
- No public awareness of or support for the partnership's work
- Lack of continuity when leadership and/or staffing changes

What follows is a discussion of major barriers facing the creation of successful partnerships and suggestions for how to navigate these predictable challenges.

Politics

Politics within and between people, educational systems, and individual schools and postsecondary institutions can easily derail the best laid plans. Getting beyond politics is particularly challenging, since there are politics within and between our educational systems. Our educational systems developed separately and have different goals, objectives, and incentives related to key organizational missions and areas such as funding, accountability, professional development, assessment, curriculum development, and other key issues. There are few universal takeaways about "getting the politics" right, but it is clear that the heads of each educational entity must lend their support publicly and be willing to defuse tough situations behind the scenes. Partnerships between high schools and postsecondary institutions will not work effectively if the leaders do not have a common vision and if they appoint the wrong people as point people.

Eliminating the "Blame Game"

The most frequent disagreement encountered during initial partnership workshops conducted by EPIC involved a tendency of institutional representatives to want to focus on the many reasons that all students are not currently college and career ready. This can quickly devolve into finger pointing and blaming others across the institutional divide. A solution for overcoming this destructive dialog is to establish, at the onset, a shared understanding that everyone— representatives from schools, colleges, businesses, and community organizations, along with parents and students—has critical contributions to make to build successful pathways that span early childhood

> Agree to avoid faultfinding, and emphasize the need for shared responsibility.

to adulthood. Agree to avoid faultfinding, and emphasize the need for shared responsibility. A group norm for partnership meetings should include an agreement to reframe the conversation away from blame to focus on the realm of possibilities and constructive problem solving to keep the partnership moving forward.

Avoiding Turf Wars

An extension of the political issues described previously is the potential for encroaching on existing areas of authority. Local or regional partnerships must agree up front not to interfere in the existing compensatory or management structures of participants. No one willingly enters into a collaboration feeling threatened (Rochford, 2007, p. 62). Any realignment of responsibilities and resources must be developed through consensus with the stakeholders so as to not create pockets of resistance and undermining of the work.

Moving Beyond Information Sharing

The danger many partnership meetings face is turning into a "show and tell" session to discuss updates about current work. The risk lies in any meeting being entirely an information session or in seeking "legitimacy by sharing" for current programs. Any meeting that brings together highly accomplished and talented individuals must be cognizant of the value of its members' time and must seek to maximize the use of that time (Rochford, 2007). Agendas should be constructed to address updates on the progress in meeting the partnership's goals, with opportunities for discussion and troubleshooting. All meetings should end with agreed on next steps with assigned responsibilities and time lines.

Ensuring Sufficient Resources

The most common additional resources needed as reported by participants in P–16 efforts were money, staffing, time, and the attention of key leaders (Walsh, 2009). Many partnership efforts fall down because "they don't have dedicated staff to do the work and so it ends up being a communications vehicle where the whole agenda is to get ready for the next meeting" (Weldon, 2009, p. 5). A crucial part of the executive leadership team's responsibilities is to secure the resources necessary to support the goals. Typical resources used to support this work include grant-based funding, workforce development/partner-based funding (to support the growth of a healthy and strong workforce), and in-kind support (in which all partners contribute staff time). This includes having partners dedicate staff time to support the planning, execution, and monitoring of the partnership's efforts. It also includes a willingness to blend resources across institutional lines. This is particularly challenging in terms of overcoming institutional silos. Integration of resources should happen over time, as trust and consensus are built to understand the necessity.

Sustainability

Ultimately, the primary challenge facing college and career readiness partnerships is sustainability. The key is to remember that partnering to improve college and career readiness is a process, not a program. As described in Chapter 5, well-intentioned educational reformers are forever in search of a silver bullet or quick programmatic fixes to systemic problems. As Rochford (2007) cautioned, "There is a danger in thinking of any P–16 [partnership] as a program. Programs have finite resources and life spans. P–16s are a process and a way of doing business" (p. 79). Thinking of a partnership as a program creates efforts that are "piecemeal, disconnected, and of short duration" (O'Banion, 2011, p. 29). Rochford eloquently described the following:

> Local and regional P–16s [partnerships] are about process. They are about building collective community awareness among principle policy makers and their organizations. They are about changing mindsets. Here, community leaders think together, even dream together, about what can be. It is the building of civic capacity. (p. 84)

The remainder of this chapter describes three foundational areas that must be addressed to achieve a sustainable process: leadership, communication, and capacity building.

Leadership is the critical foundation for sustaining successful partnerships. In a four-state study, the Partnerships for Student Success found that strong leadership directed toward collaborative work appeared to make a significant difference in terms of creating the support and energy necessary to move the agenda forward and create sustainable change. Leadership was found to create opportunities for reform, set parameters, embed policies, and create innovative reforms (Rochford, 2007). For leadership, three types of roles are critical:

1. *Decision makers:* Leaders with the power to set priorities and make resource and staffing decisions. For example, a strong criticism of P–16 councils is the lack of authority to enact and implement policies. Councils without decision-making authority "often are little more than communication vehicles, rather than policy tools to produce real and lasting results" (Weldon, 2009, p. 1).

2. *Implementers:* "Boundary scanners" skilled in working across professional organizational or other boundaries to overcome departmental and institutional silos (Wildridge et al., 2004, p. 7).

3. *Champions:* Community advocates to generate and maintain support and serve as ambassadors for the college and career readiness efforts (Rochford, 2007, p. 8).

To sustain the partnership, leadership capacity must grow over time. This includes identifying, growing, and supporting peer leaders to continue the work to address the reality of staff turnover.

Clear and consistent communication is another critical element of success for sustainability. This includes not only the sharing of critical and timely information but the active inclusion of stakeholder perspectives. Participants must feel heard to remain committed (Wildridge et al., 2004). One clear strain of work needs to be the development of a communication strategy. This strategy should address why college and career readiness is critical for students and the future of the community, what the goals of the partnership are, and how community members should be involved. A communications task force should be formed for crafting the message, developing the marketing materials, and engaging the delivery chain for the ongoing process of keeping up with changing issues and levels of understanding. A delivery chain includes key leaders and boundary scanners that serve as ambassadors that deliver the messaging and important information to all of the various key stakeholder groups, including students, parents, educators, policymakers, business representatives, community members, and the media. The communications team is not only responsible for developing the messaging and marketing materials and activating the delivery chain but also for establishing a feedback loop involving key stakeholders to monitor and refine the communications strategy.

Examples of Communication Activities

- Build a distribution list for information and regular updates.
- Publish a periodic newsletter on the website and send it via an email distribution list.
- Schedule regular one-on-one briefings and check-ins with key stakeholders.
- Partner to identify participant leaders in networks and peer working groups.
- Identify and send targeted information to ambassadors to be delivered at the grassroots level (including classrooms).
- Designate informed "ambassadors" for peer-to-peer messaging.
- Schedule presentations at group meetings throughout the community.
- Disseminate and collect feedback about informational resources that have been developed.
- Involve unions, faculty committees, and community organizations in the distribution process.
- Schedule frequent presentations at all applicable meetings.
- Organize regional informational sessions.
- Identify, utilize, and grow existing educator networks.
- Engage the media: Write op-ed pieces and letters to the editor, meet with editorial boards, provide press releases, and schedule briefings.
- Leverage social media to blast out updates.
- Develop feedback mechanisms, such as school climate surveys, key stakeholder interviews, and meeting evaluation forms.

Leadership and communication build relationships. Relationships build capacity to undergo deep and sustained reform efforts. For successful partnerships, this translates to the building of collaborative capacity. Foster-Fishman et al. (2001) identified four levels of collaborative capacity to build sustainable community change:

- Member Capacity: A partnership's membership is widely regarded as its primary asset, and success depends on the extent to which its members have the capacity to perform needed tasks and work collaboratively together.
- Relational Capacity: Stakeholder relationships (both internally and externally) provide the medium for collaborative work and facilitate access to needed resources; promote the stakeholder commitment, satisfaction, and involvement needed to successfully pursue collaborative endeavors; foster viability; and increase the likelihood that partnership efforts will be sustained long term.

- Organizational Capacity: Ultimately, if a partnership is to survive, it must have the organizational capacity to engage stakeholders in needed work tasks to produce desired products and transform individual interests into a dynamic collective force that achieves targeted outcomes.
- Programmatic Capacity: Partnerships need the capacity to guide the design and implementation of programs that have real, meaningful impact within their communities. The actual role partnerships play in implementing new programs varies considerably, with some actually implementing the programs themselves and others playing more of a catalyst role, using existing organizations to implement these initiatives.

Collaborative capacity needs to be fostered and expanded over time. Addressing all four levels of capacity needs to be an explicit part of the partnership process by the leadership team and by any additional task forces established to support various efforts. Just as monitoring and accountability need to be part of the ongoing partnership work, so does collaboration.

Overall, significant and lasting change, as described by Fullan (2001), is the process of creating shared meaning across a group of people working in concert. This process is undergirded by a shared "moral commitment, knowledge creation, and program coherence" supported by organizational changes "necessary to provide supportive or stimulating conditions to foster change in practice" (pp. 47–48). The creation of shared intellectual and moral meaning is not about "making individuals 'feel better' but is fundamentally related to whether teachers [or other participants] are likely to find the considerable energy required to transform the status quo" (p. 48). Civic capacity—the capacity to collectively set goals and effectively pursue them (Henig, Hula, Orr, & Pedescleaux, 1999)—underscores the intergroup relationships necessary to create the shared meaning necessary for real and lasting change. In the end, effective college and career readiness partnerships foster the civic capacity necessary to transcend entrenched interests to enable every student to be prepared to achieve their postsecondary aspirations.

> In the end, effective college and career readiness partnerships foster the civic capacity necessary to transcend entrenched interests to enable every student to be prepared to achieve their postsecondary aspirations.

Conclusion

There is no single recipe to follow that will create a successful college and career readiness partnership. This book has mapped out the following process to help partners work together to develop an approach that will build on the unique assets and meet the needs of each unique context:

    I. Develop a shared understanding of college and career readiness (Chapter 1).

    II. Use the Four Keys to College and Career Readiness as a guiding framework (Chapter 2).

    III. Establish leadership (Chapter 3).

    IV. Develop a vision and goals (Chapter 3).

    V. Select an organizing structure or model (Chapter 3).

    VI. Create a College and Career Readiness culture (Chapters 3 and 5).

    VII. Select measures of success (Chapter 4).

        a. Determine indicators and outcome measures.

        b. Evaluate and self-assess efforts.

    VIII. Plan for action (Chapter 5).

        a. Identify and map existing efforts.

        b. Create an implementation plan, including strategies and activities addressing all Four Keys for all students.

    IX. Align curricula across educational systems (Chapter 6).

        a. Share existing curricula.

        b. Conduct a gap analysis.

        c. Align content.

        d. Calibrate student performance expectations.

        e. Direct ongoing updates and refinements.

    X. Sustain the work (Chapter 7).

        a. Leadership

        b. Communication

        c. Capacity

Each community must foster a partnership built on its strengths and priorities. There are several themes that run through this book that are worth repeating when embarking on the work of creating an effective college and career readiness partnership:

- *College and career readiness is for all students.* This does not mean that all students will go directly to college or that all students will enroll in a degree program. Students need to be prepared to learn in whatever setting they choose beyond high school. The focus of this book is on readiness for additional education or training beyond high school—not just a traditional bachelor's degree. The partnership work needs to support all students, and the programming and data need to be analyzed by subgroups to make sure that students are not overlooked and do not have gaps in their learning and opportunities.

- *Partnering is a process, not a program.* There is no magic bullet that will instantly make all students college and career ready. Success will be incremental, involving multiple steps and differing levels of involvement over time. The process must be organized, intentionally managed, and supported by leadership.

- *Engage in possibility thinking.* Do not let partnership efforts get bogged down in finding blame or rehashing old failures. Learn from and build on the past, but keep the focus on the future and what can be done. A favorite phrase used by EPIC to redirect stalled conversations is this: "Share your best innovation thinking—what should we be doing?"

- *Do not wait for permission from above.* Local communities do not need to wait for permission from the state or federal government to form partnerships. Many of the systems' issues do stem from above, but local schools and colleges can partner with the community to improve local student outcomes, with the freedom to focus on local needs and priorities.

- *Do not reinvent the wheel.* Much of this work has been done before, albeit with different contexts or purposes. Learn from others. Information is readily available in a way that it never has been. Although this book contains many examples, the struggle was with narrowing down all there is available to share. Explore and choose, and alter and transform to meet local needs. This expedites the process and helps to reduce avoidable problems by learning from the lessons of others.

In the end, this partnership work is really about the key stakeholders in a community coming together so that youth are prepared to have successful futures. Partnerships help adults see beyond their own institutional settings and work together to solve a complex developmental process that transcends institutional boundaries. Most importantly, the college and career readiness partnerships described in this book occur at the local level. This is the level that directly interacts with and impacts students' lives and can prepare all students for success beyond high school.

SUMMARY

P–20 partnership work is primarily about building and sustaining relationships and trust; relationships across systems have few incentives to develop, scarce resources, layers of politics, and deep historical disconnects. The constant churn of educational policy has created an environment in which leaders and their staff come and go, making it challenging to forge lasting relationships, and efforts are often fractured by funding streams. Getting beyond politics can be particularly difficult, since our educational systems developed separately and have different goals, objectives, and incentives related to key organizational missions. To be most successful, the tools and strategies need to be used in environments in which the relationships are on solid footing, with agreement on key goals and objectives. The chapter discusses typical land mines, or challenges, that face many partnerships. When it comes to sustainability, key issues to remember include maintaining the focus on achieving the vision and not on assigning blame; engaging in possibility thinking by focusing on what can be done; remembering that partnering to improve college and career readiness is a process, not a program or policy; and learning and adapting from the work of others.

DISCUSSION QUESTIONS

- Does your partnership have a clear sense of its challenges (such as politics, blaming, turf battles, and funding)? Does the leadership acknowledge those issues and work with partners to make significant headway to remove barriers?
- What kinds of communication channels does your partnership use? Do you think those channels are effective? Based on what kind of evidence?

- Does your partnership have enough capacity? If it is lacking capacity, where does it most need to build capacity (member, relational, organizational, programmatic)?
- Is your partnership dependent on specific individuals for continuity? How can buy-in and responsibilities be more universally shared?
- How will the partnership monitor the effectiveness of the work in achieving the goals? How will changes be decided?

References

Allen, L., & Murphy, L. (2008). *Leveraging postsecondary partners to build a college-going culture: Tools for high school/postsecondary partnership.* Boston, MA: Jobs For the Future. Retrieved from http://www.jff.org/sites/default/files/publications/materials/ToolsPSEpshipslowres_2.pdf

Bailey, T., & Cho, S-W. (2010). *Developmental education in community colleges.* Community College Research Center Issue Brief prepared for the White House Summit on Community Colleges. New York, NY: Columbia University Teachers College.

Barnett, W., Corrin, W., Nakanishi, A., Bork, R., Mitchell, C., & Sepanik, S. (2012). *Preparing high school students for college: An exploratory study of college readiness partnership programs in Texas.* New York, NY: National Center for Postsecondary Research. Retrieved from http://www.tc.columbia.edu/i/a/document/22458_NCPR_CRPFullReport_051712.pdf

Bernstein, K. (2013). Warnings from the trenches. *American Association of University Professors.* Retrieved from http://www.aaup.org/article/warnings-trenches#.UehKXpVoa0s

The California State University. (n.d.). Early Assessment Program. Retrieved from http://www.calstate.edu/eap

Carnevale, A., Jayasundera, T., & Cheah, B. (2012). *The college advantage: Weathering the economic storm.* Washington, DC: The Georgetown University Center on Education and the Workforce. Retrieved from https://georgetown.app.box.com/s/cwmx7i5li1nxd7zt7mim

Carnevale, A., Rose, S., & Cheah, B. (2011). *The college payoff: Education, occupations, lifetime earnings.* Washington, DC: The Georgetown University Center on Education and the Workforce. Retrieved from https://cew.georgetown.edu/report/the-college-payoff/

Carnevale, A., Smith, N., & Strohl, J. (2010). *Help wanted: Projections of jobs and education requirements through 2018.* Washington, DC: The Georgetown University Center on Education and the Workforce. Retrieved from https://cew.georgetown.edu/report/help-wanted/

Casner-Lotto, J., & Benner, M. (2006). *Are they really ready to work: Employers' perspectives on the basic knowledge and applied skills of new entrants to the 21st century U.S. workforce.* Consortium Report from the Conference Board, Corporate Voices for Working Families, Partnership for 21st Century Skills, and Society for Human Resource Management. Retrieved from http://www.p21.org/storage/documents/FINAL_REPORT_PDF09-29-06.pdf

Collins, S., Davis-Molin, W., McGaughy, C., & Conley, D. (2013). *South Carolina accountability review and revision: An analytical framework.* Eugene, OR: Educational Policy Improvement Center. Retrieved from http://www.epiconline.org/publications/south-carolina-accountability-review-revision-an-analytical-framework

Conley, D. (2005). *College knowledge: What it really takes for students to succeed and what we can do to get them ready.* San Francisco, CA: Jossey-Bass.

Conley, D. (2010). *College and career ready: Helping all students succeed beyond high school.* San Francisco, CA: Jossey-Bass.

Conley, D. (2013). *College, career, and the Common Core.* San Francisco, CA: Jossey-Bass.

Conley, D., Drummond, K., de Gonzalez, A., Rooseboom, J., & Stout, O. (2011a). *Reaching the goal: The applicability and importance of the Common Core State Standards to college and career readiness.* Eugene, OR: Educational Policy Improvement Center. Retrieved from https://www.epiconline.org/publications/documents/ReachingtheGoal-FullReport.pdf

Conley, D., Drummond, K., de Gonzalez, A., Seburn, M., Stout, O., & Rooseboom, J. (2011b). *Lining up: The relationship between the Common Core State Standards and five sets of comparison standards.* Eugene, OR: Educational Policy Improvement Center. Retrieved from http://www.epiconline.org/publications/documents/LiningUp-FullReport_2011.pdf

Conley, D., & McGaughy, C. (2012). College and career readiness: Same or different? *Educational Leadership, 69*(7), 28–34.

Conley, D., McGaughy, C., Brown, D., van der Valk, A., & Young, B. (2009). *Validation study III: Alignment of the Texas College and Career Readiness Standards with courses in two career pathways.* Eugene, OR: Educational Policy Improvement Center.

Conley, D., McGaughy, C., Cadigan, K., Forbes, J., Martinez, M., & Young, B. (2009). *Texas College and Career Readiness Standards Regional Meetings Final Report.* Prepared on behalf of the Texas Higher Education Coordinating Board. Eugene, OR: Educational Policy Improvement Center.

Conley, D., McGaughy, C., Ward, T., & Martinez, M. (2008). *Massachusetts Regional Alignment Workshops: Final Report.* Prepared on behalf of the Commonwealth of Massachusetts Department of Elementary and Secondary Education. Eugene, OR: Educational Policy Improvement Center. Retrieved from http://www.epiconline.org/publications/documents/2008_MA_Regional_Alignment_FinalReport.pdf

Council of Chief State School Officers & National Governors Association. (2011). *Common Core State Standards Initiative.* Retrieved from http://www.corestandards.org

Crowson, R., & Boyd, W. (1996). Structure and strategies: Toward an understanding of alternative models for coordinated children's services. In J. Cibulka & W. Kritek (Eds.), *Coordination among schools, families, and communities: Prospects for education reform* (pp. 137–169). Albany: State University of New York Press.

Dadgar, M., Nodine, T., Bracco, K., & Venezia, A. (2013). *Integrating student supports and academics.* San Francisco, CA: WestEd. Retrieved from careers.wested.org/cs/we/view/rs/1296

Data Quality Campaign. (2014). *Data FAQs.* Washington, DC: Data Quality Campaign. Retrieved from http://www.dataqualitycampaign.org/why-education-data/data-faqs

Duncan, A. (2013, June 25). Duncan pushes back on attacks on Common Core Standards. Arne Duncan remarks at the American Society of News Editors annual convention, Capital Hilton, Washington, DC. Retrieved from http://www.ed.gov/news/speeches/duncan-pushes-back-attacks-common-core-standards

The Education Trust. (2010). *Shut out of the military: Today's high school education doesn't mean you're ready for today's army.* Retrieved from http://edtrust.org/resource/shut-out-of-the-military-todays-high-school-education-doesnt-mean-youre-ready-for-todays-army/

Educational Policy Improvement Center (EPIC). (2007). *South Carolina Course Alignment Project: Environmental Scan.* Prepared on behalf of the South Carolina Commission on Higher Education. Eugene, OR: Educational Policy Improvement Center. Retrieved from http://www.epiconline.org/publications/documents/SC_EnviroScan_lorez.pdf

Foster-Fishman, P., Berkowitz, S., Lounsbury, D., Jacobson, S., & Allen, N. (2001). Building collaborative capacity in community coalitions: A review and integrative framework. *American Journal of Community Psychology, 29*(2), 241–261.

Foundation for Excellence in Education. (2013). *Common Core State Standards information: Common misconceptions.* Retrieved from http://excelined.org/common-core-toolkit/information-common-misconceptions/

Fullan, M. (2001). *Leading in a culture of change.* San Francisco, CA: Jossey-Bass.

Gabriel, J., & Farmer, P. (2009). *How to help your school thrive without breaking the bank.* Alexandria, VA: Association for Supervision and Curriculum Development. Retrieved from http://www.ascd.org/publications/books/107042/chapters/developing-a-vision-and-a-mission.aspx

Goldring, E. B., Cohen-Vogel, L., & Smrekar, C. (2003). *Neighborhood capacity in the postbusing era: What does "closer to home" mean for families and schools?* Paper presented at the annual meeting of the American Educational Research Association, Chicago, IL.

Henig, J., Hula, R., Orr, M., & Pedescleaux, D. (1999). *The color of school reform: Race, politics and the challenge of urban education.* Princeton, NJ: Princeton University Press.

Imperial County Office of Education. (n.d.). P16 Council. Retrieved from http://www.icoe.org/educational/college-going-initiative/p-16-council

John W. Gardner Center. (2014). *Menu of college readiness indicators and supports.* College Readiness Indicator Systems Resource Series. Seattle, WA: Bill & Melinda Gates Foundation. Retrieved from http://gardnercenter.stanford.edu/resources/publications/Menu.CRIS.pdf

Karp, M., O'Gara, L., & Hughes, K. (2008). *Do support services at community colleges encourage success or reproduce disadvantage? An exploratory study of students in two community colleges* (CCRC Working Paper No. 10). New York, NY: Community College Research Center (CCRC), Teachers College, Columbia University. Retrieved from ccrc.tc.columbia.edu/publications/do-support-services-encourage-success.html

Kirst, M., & Usdan, M. (2009). Chapter 1: The historical context of the divide between K–12 and higher education. In *States, schools, and colleges: Polices to improve student readiness for college and strengthen coordination between schools and colleges* (pp. 5–22). San Jose, CA: The National Center for Public Policy and Higher Education. Retrieved from http://www.highereducation.org/reports/ssc/ssc_k16.pdf

Krueger, C. (2006, April). *The progress of P-16 collaboration in the states.* Denver, CO: Education Commission of the States.

Kuther, T. (2013, September). What employers seek in job applicants: You've got the skills they want. *Psychology Student Network.* Washington, DC: American Psychological Association. Retrieved from http://www.apa.org/ed/precollege/psn/2013/09/job-applicants.aspx

Lindsey, G., Todd, J. A., & Hayter, S. (2009, September). *A handbook for planning and conducting charrettes for high-performance projects* (2nd ed.). Golden, CO: National Renewable Energy Laboratory. Retrieved from http://www.nrel.gov/docs/fy09osti/44051.pdf

Los Angeles Community College District. (2015). *Our colleges.* Los Angeles, CA: Los Angeles Community College District. Retrieved from https://www.laccd.edu/About/Pages/Our-Colleges.aspx

Los Angeles Unified School District. (n.d.). Los Angeles Unified School District Profile. Los Angeles, CA: Office of Data and Accountability, School Information Branch, Los Angeles Unified School District. Retrieved from http://search.lausd.k12.ca.us/cgi-bin/fccgi.exe?w3exec=school0

McDonough, P. (1997). *Choosing colleges: How social class and schools structure opportunity.* Albany, NY: State University of New York Press.

McGaughy, C., van der Valk, A., Singleton, J., Zalewski, T., & Farkas, R. (2012). *Bridging the gap: An Illinois toolkit for using the Common Core for secondary and postsecondary alignment.* Eugene, OR: Educational Policy Improvement Center. Retrieved from http://www.epiconline.org/publications/documents/IL_Toolkit_v2_FINAL_reduced.pdf

Moore, C., Venezia, A., & Lewis, J. (March 2015). Organizing for success: California's regional partnerships. Sacramento, CA: Education Insights Center. Retrieved from http://www.csus.edu/edinsights/PDFs/R_OrganizingForSuccess_0315.pdf

MPR Associates, Inc. (2010). *Programs of study: Local implementation readiness and capacity for self-assessment: A tool for local college and career readiness.* Prepared for the Office of Vocational and Adult Education, U.S. Department of Education. Berkeley, CA: MPR Associates, Inc. Retrieved from http://cte.ed.gov/docs/POSLocalImplementationTool-9-14-10.pdf

Nanus, B. (1992). *Visionary leadership: Creating a compelling sense of direction for your organization.* San Francisco, CA: Jossey-Bass.

National Center for Education Statistics (NCES). (2008). Common Core Data, IPEDS Residency and Migration Survey, IPEDS Enrollment Survey, IPEDS Graduation Rate Survey. Retrieved from http://www.higheredinfo.org/dbrowser/index.php?submeasure=119&year=2008&level=nation&mode=data&state=0

National Leadership Council for Liberal Education & America's Promise. (2007). *College learning for the new global century.* Washington, DC: Association of American Colleges and Universities. Retrieved from http://www.aacu.org/leap/documents/GlobalCentury_final.pdf

Oakes, J. (2005). *Keeping track: How schools structure inequality* (2nd ed.). New Haven, CT: Yale University Press.

O'Banion, T. (2011). Pathways to completion: Guidelines to boosting student success. *Community College Journal, 82*(1), 28–34.

Offenstein, J., Moore, C., & Shulock, N. (2010, May 6). *Advancing by degrees.* Washington, DC: The Education Trust.

Owen, S., & Sawhill, I. (2013). *Should everyone go to college?* (Center on Children and Families Issue Brief No. 50). Washington, DC: The Brookings Institution. Retrieved from http://www.brookings.edu/~/media/ research/files/papers/2013/05/07%20should%20everyone%20go%20 to%20college%20owen%20sawhill/08%20should%20everyone%20 go%20to%20college%20owen%20sawhill.pdf

Rochford, J. (2007). P-16: *The last education reform. Book Two: Emerging local, regional, and state efforts.* Canton, OH: Stark Education Partnership.

Rosenbaum, J., Stephan, J., & Rosenbaum J. (2010). Beyond one-size-fits-all college dreams: Alternative pathways to desirable careers. *American Educator, 34*(3), 2–8, 10–13. Retrieved from http://www.aft.org/pdfs/ americaneducator/fall2010/Rosenbaum.pdf

Sambolt, M., & Balestreri, K. (2013, December). *Considerations to support college and career readiness: A facilitator's guide.* Washington, DC: College & Career Readiness & Success Center, American Institutes for Research.

Samuelson, R. J. (2012, May 27). It's time to drop the college-for-all crusade. *The Washington Post.* Retrieved from http://articles.washingtonpost .com/2012-05-27/opinions/35456501_1_college-students-josipa-roksa- private-colleges-and-universities

Schaid, J. (2014, April 24). *Elgin Community College's Alliance for College Readiness: Building effective partnerships & transition stages.* Paper presented at the workshop of STEM College and Career Readiness: Partners in Readiness, Illinois Community College Board, Elgin. Retrieved from http://icsps.illi noisstate.edu/wp-content/uploads/2014/04/Schaid.Elgin_.Panel_-2.pdf

Schleicher, A. (2010). The case for 21st-century learning. *Organisation for Economic Co-operation and Development (OECD).* Retrieved from http:// www.oecd.org/general/thecasefor21st-centurylearning.htm

Scolari, L., & Antrobus, R. (2014). *Self-assessment of an effective community college/K-12 partnership.* Oakland, CA: Career Ladders Project for California Community Colleges. Retrieved from http://www.career laddersproject.org/wp-content/uploads/2014/01/H2C-Partnership- Self-Assessment-Tool2.pdf

Smrekar, C., & Mawhinney, H. (1999). Integrated services: Challenges in linking schools, families, and communities. In J. Murphy & K. Louis (Eds.), *Handbook of research of educational administration* (2nd ed., pp. 443–461). San Francisco, CA: Jossey-Bass.

Strauss, V. (2013, April 19). Common Core Standards attacked by republicans. *The Washington Post.* Retrieved from http://www.washingtonpost .com/blogs/answer-sheet/wp/2013/04/19/common-core-standards- attacked-by-republicans/

Symonds, W., Schwartz, R., & Ferguson, R. (2011, February). *Pathways to prosperity: Meeting the challenge of preparing young Americans for the 21st century* (Report issued by the Pathways to Prosperity Project, Harvard Graduate School of Education). Retrieved from http://dash.harvard.edu/bitstream/ handle/1/4740480/Pathways_to_Prosperity_Feb2011-1.pdf?sequence=1

University of Chicago Consortium on Chicago School Research. (2014). *Selecting effective indicators.* College Readiness Indicator Systems Resource Series. Seattle, WA: Bill & Melinda Gates Foundation. Retrieved from http://ccsr.uchicago.edu/sites/default/files/publications/Selecting Indicators.CRIS_.pdf

U.S. Department of Education (U.S. DoED). (2015, January 27). Student Support Services Program. Washington, DC: US DoED. Retrieved from http://www2.ed.gov/programs/triostudsupp/index.html

Van Horn, C., Zukin, C., Szeltner, M., & Stone, C. (2012). *Left out. Forgotten? Recent high school graduates and the great recession. Work trends.* New Brunswick, NJ: Rutgers, The State University of New Jersey, John J. Heldrich Center for Workforce Development. Retrieved from http://files.eric.ed.gov/fulltext/ED535271.pdf

Van Roekel, D. (2013, January 7). *Getting to the core of Common Core: Change is hard—not necessarily bad.* National Education Association. Retrieved from http://www.nea.org/home/53977.htm

Venezia, A., Bracco, K., & Nodine, T. (2010). *One-shot deal? Students' perceptions of assessment and course placement in California's community colleges.* San Francisco, CA: WestEd. Retrieved from http://www.wested.org/online_pubs/oneshotdeal.pdf

Venezia, A., Callan, P., Finney, J., Kirst, M., & Usdan, M. (2005, September). *The governance divide: A report on a four-state study on improving college readiness and success* (The National Center for Public Policy and Higher Education Report no. 05-3). Retrieved from http://www.highereducation.org/reports/governance_divide/

Venezia, A., Kirst, M. W., & Antonio, A. L. (2003). *Betraying the college dream: How disconnected K-12 and postsecondary education systems undermine student aspirations.* Stanford, CA: Stanford Institute for Higher Education Research.

Walsh, E. J. (2009, November). Chapter 2: P-16 policy alignment in the states: Findings from a 50-state survey. In *States, schools, and colleges: Policies to improve student readiness for college and strengthen coordination between schools and colleges* (pp. 23–34). San Jose, CA: The National Center for Public Policy and Higher Education. Retrieved from http://www.highereducation.org/reports/ssc/ssc_k16.pdf

Webb, N. L. (1997). *Criteria for alignment of expectations and assessments in mathematics and science education.* Council of Chief State School Officers & National Institute for Science Education (Research Monograph No. 6). Madison: University of Wisconsin, Wisconsin Center for Education Research.

Weissman, E., Cerna, O., Geckeler, C., Schneider, E., Price, D., & Smith, T. (2009, July). *Promoting partnerships for student success: Lesson from the SSPIRE Initiative.* New York, NY: MDRC. Retrieved from http://www.mdrc.org/publication/promoting-partnerships-student-success

Weldon, T. (2009). P-16/20 school governance: A trends in America special report. *The Council of State Governments.* Retrieved from http://www.csg.org/knowledgecenter/docs/TIA_Focus_P16%20Councils.pdf

Wier, K. (2013). Feel like a fraud? *gradPSYCH, 11*(4), 24. Washington, DC: American Psychological Association. Retrieved from http://www.apa.org/gradpsych/2013/11/fraud.aspx

Wildridge, V., Childs, S., Cawthra, L., & Madge, B. (2004). How to create successful partnerships—A review of the literature. *Health Information and Libraries Journal, 21,* 3–19.

Index

A SAGE Company

CORWIN HAS ONE MISSION: to enhance education through intentional professional learning.

We build long-term relationships with our authors, educators, clients, and associations who partner with us to develop and continuously improve the best evidence-based practices that establish and support lifelong learning.